The Pathway to the Father's Heart

Discovering True Identity

TERRINA WILDER

Published by Terrina Wilder
www.terrinawilder.com

Library of Congress Cataloging-in-Publication Data is available upon request.

ISBN (eBook): 978-1-64184-067-5
ISBN (paperback): 978-1-64184-068-2
ISBN (hardback): 978-1-64184-069-9

DEDICATION

This book is being dedicated to my first love, my heavenly Father. As such, I share the following prayer:

Lord, I surrender my desires over to You. I trust that my desires, whether fulfilled in my timing or not, will not cause me to think I have failed. You must be my main focus. I know You want me to prosper and be successful, but I don't want to lose sight of You or Your hand. Draw me close to You. Lord, You say I must depend on You, and You'll show me the way to go. I need You, Father, to direct me, to direct my thoughts and the desires for this new season of life.

May You continue to be on my mind early in the morning and when I retire for the evening. When I seek You, let me find You. I am convinced that there is power and authority in my prayers. I thank You for showing me how to love. Continue to work on my heart, Lord. You have never failed me! You have modeled Yourself as the perfect husband and confidant, and I praise Your Most Holy Name. Amen.

CONTENTS

ACKNOWLEDGMENTS

There are so many people to thank who have helped me in completing this biography. I first want to thank my dear friend Alicia Braxton for taking the time out of her busy schedule to encourage me and offer her honest perspective when mine was a little off-centered.

My family, we have experienced so much in life together or merely by association. It still amazes me how God designed our family. My hope is that we will grow in His love to, in turn, love each other as He has called us to do. I do love you all and desire God's best for your lives. May the covenant of His peace be upon each of you for many generations to come.

To the counselors at Denton County Friends of the Family and Deliverance Prayer Ministers at Mining the Truth and Never Gives Up Ministries, thank you for helping me navigate through areas where healing from deep emotional and spiritual wounding had occurred. I've experienced such freedom in being who I truly am to live life with godly purpose.

To my fellow Christian sisters and brothers—Tara Kreuger, Sonia Mayeaux Morales, Craig Groshans, and so many others — who extended compassion, love, patience, and kindness to me as I waited to hear the DNA test results or walked alongside me during very low periods. Proverbs 27:17 is very true: *As iron sharpens iron, so a man sharpens the countenance of his friend.* Your impact on my life is priceless; it's eternal. Thank you so much!

INTRODUCTION

My story, while unique to me, is in many regards similar to what thousands have experienced in their lives.

I grew up in a large midwestern community while neither knowing my biological father nor having any significant relationships with other adult men. I struggled with poor self-esteem and feelings of loneliness and abandonment.

It wasn't the solid foundation for a good life that I would have built, but the experience shaped me into the woman I am today. In retrospect, my early childhood opened the door for God to step in and become my Father. He orchestrated opportunities and divine appointments with people who came into my life to either teach me a lesson, help me grow personally, or point me toward the next steps I needed to take.

I love my parents, both my mother and my stepfather. I have a great deal of respect for them because they did the best they could with what they had. Their own upbringing was less than stellar, and the insecurities and doubts they brought into adulthood shaped their worldview and how they would parent me and my siblings.

Growing up without my biological father in my life left a gaping wound, as though a part of me was missing. I longed for a relationship with him and looked forward to the day I would eventually meet him—something I was forbidden to do. Yet it happened shortly after I graduated from college.

A series of disappointments and stressful relationships left me guarding my heart to protect it from further heartbreak. I was determined to not let anyone get close enough to hurt me again.

While the independence I displayed for the world to see

enabled me to become a strong, confident woman, it also left me secretly longing for a type of love that I had yet to experience.

As I grew older, I ventured on a journey to salve those wounds and insecurities in order to prove to myself and others that I was fully capable of achieving a successful life despite my shattered start. I achieved things that others my age were unable to attain; yet there was a brokenness that always seemed to surface at just the right time to block whatever progress I was trying to make.

Those troubles forced me to press in even closer to a relationship I formed with my heavenly Father—rather He forged with me—who promised me repeatedly that He would never leave me nor forsake me. He promised to be more than just a cheerleader, but rather the God of infinite possibilities and unbroken promises. As I learned to trust God more, amazing things began to happen in my life.

He brought restoration not only to my life but also to the relationship I now enjoy with my earthly father. He has opened doors and shined a lamp onto my feet to guide my steps. I wasn't always obedient to His prompting, but He loved me anyway and kept me from becoming a recluse until I was ready to admit that His way was best.

Many of the names have been changed, and as you read this book, I invite you to share my journey—to cry as I cried, to contemplate the choices I was required to make, to celebrate as I experienced victory, and to bask in a love I discovered that is so profound, so vast, and so incredibly genuine that it overshadows any longings that remain in my heart.

My God is my superhero, leading me from one personal victory to another, all the while assuring me that if I seek Him first, He will continue to fulfill every desire of my heart because my heart will be closely aligned with His.

CHAPTER 1

Early Life

For You formed my inward parts; You covered me in my mother's womb. I will praise You, for I am fearfully and wonderfully made; marvelous are Your works, and that my soul knows very well. My frame was not hidden from You, when I was made in secret, and skillfully wrought in the lowest parts of the earth. Your eyes saw my substance, being yet unformed. And in Your book they all were written, the days fashioned for me, when as yet there were none of them.

—Ps. 139:13–16

I was born in Milwaukee, Wisconsin. It is a large industrial city along the shores of Lake Michigan and a few hours north of Chicago. Milwaukee was immortalized in television shows like Laverne & Shirley and Happy Days.

When my mother was just sixteen years old and in high school, she became pregnant with my sister, Rose. My mother dropped out of high school and would later return to school to get her GED. She truly desired to get ahead in life with the hope of having a career, a house of her own, and someone to share her life with one day.

Rose's father never married my mother. After all, he was just a teenager himself when my sister was born. During those early years, my mother and sister lived with my grandmother, who we called "Grandmo." Grandmo had hoped my mother would finish high school, land a good job, and settle down with a good man.

Prior to me arriving only three years later, my mother would have her own rented place before her twentieth birthday.

My mother and father met during a time when she was trying to move on from a relationship she had with Patrick, who would later become my stepfather. Randolph, my father, was nineteen and considered to be a father-like figure to his younger siblings back in Louisiana. He was very giving in his finances, and this trait would often make him a target for others to abuse.

At some point, my mother and father clashed and ended their relationship before she even knew she was pregnant with me. I think my mother felt she had disappointed Grandmo and regretted being pregnant by a man she really didn't love. Randolph would learn in a painful way that my mother was still in love with Patrick. Unfortunately, harsh words were exchanged privately and publicly between the two, which had a direct impact on Randolph having a role in my life.

I grew up in a blue-collar, middle-class neighborhood where both parents generally worked jobs to help make ends meet. Many of the families near us were intact with both mother and father living at home and sharing responsibilities of raising their children, although they may not necessarily have been married. If the biological father was absent, there was generally a father figure living in the home.

One of my best friends, Crystal, lived next door with her mother and father. But the neighbors on the other side of our house were an older couple who were raising several of their grandchildren. I don't remember where the grandchildren's parents were.

Crystal was the only girl I really knew who had a father living in the home, and he scared me because he never smiled. He was pleasant to me, but something about him scared me, so I never viewed him as approachable or as a nurturing father.

Crystal was younger than I was by four or five years. We both loved playing with dolls and we would retreat into this land of make-believe until I was eleven years old. Some would say I was too old to play with dolls at eleven, but I really enjoyed escaping into a world where I could create and control life's outcome. Playing with dolls allowed me to do just that. We would push our dolls in buggies in the neighborhood talking to them as though they were real and making up stories about their lives.

I had one black, slender Barbie doll, and she was the mother to two medium-sized white dolls which I claimed to be the black doll's daughters. I never had a problem with interracial families, even as a young girl, so I didn't find this mother-daughter mix to be unusual.

I can't remember what I named my dolls, but I remember I created a social life for them where they would go to parties or on special outings while being careful to love, support, and encourage one another. Beauty was a big thing for me, so I would take special care to make sure their hair looked perfect along with their clothes.

Looking back, I was imagining a family I desired to have in real life. I would nurture the dolls like I longed to be nurtured myself. The funny thing was that there wasn't a man involved in this fantasy family. As a child, I never really appreciated the value of having a man in my life.

My parents were never married, and my sister and I had different fathers. My mother and Patrick lived together before they would marry when my brother, Tommy, was just a toddler. I was six years old when they got married, but Patrick had lived in the house for a few years before then.

My mother and I got along well. As a young child, I would call her "Mama," and later changed that to just "Ma." Patrick, on the other hand, was the father figure that I knew and identified with, but we never had a *real* relationship. When it came to raising me, he was pretty much hands-off. We rarely spoke to each other. After they were married, I was told I could call Patrick 'Daddy', but he never did any daddy-type activities with me or my sister. There was no way I could ever crawl onto his lap and just snuggle. This is a gesture I associated with bonding to a father.

Patrick had his challenges in life and coped with them the best way he knew how—even with heavy drinking. He would often lose his balance and break furniture or burn food while cooking when he was intoxicated. As a little girl, I thought he was being funny, like a clown, and I would laugh at him. I did not yet understand what alcoholism was about or the effect it had on people caught in its grip.

We got along fine when I was very young, and he would occasionally babysit me and my sister. But I don't have any memories of him being parental, like reading me books or telling me stories about when he was a child. He never shared his viewpoint regarding any topic, and he never openly offered me advice. Whenever I'd ask for his advice, he'd say, "Go ask your mother."

I suspect that Daddy and Ma had an agreement that he would never discipline my sister and me since he wasn't our *real* father. If I ever acted up, he never said a word at the time. But as soon as my mother got home, he'd tell her about my conduct, then I'd get punished.

It was very confusing for me as a young child. I'd be sound asleep when Ma would come home from work, open our bedroom door, and start spanking me with a belt for something I did hours earlier. Many times I wondered why I was being punished by her instead of Daddy.

Daddy wouldn't even scold me if I did something wrong. He was never someone I could really talk to or share my deepest fears or greatest dreams with. He had a speech impediment that caused him to stutter, and that made him very self-conscious.

He would turn to alcohol to boost his confidence. Often he

would simply drink quietly and observe from the sideline as others talked around him. He was not an angry drunk, and he never hit me, my mother, or my sister. My brother, I felt, had a more intimate relationship with Daddy, as they would often go fishing and do yard work together. He imparted more life skills into Tommy, as well as manly advice. Perhaps this was because it was easier for Daddy to bond with a male.

He rarely had direct conversation with me, even if we were sitting an arm's length away. He would always ask my mother or another adult to ask me a question or relay something to me. Conversations would become increasingly more awkward as I became an adult.

My fondest memory of spending time with Daddy took place when I was just four or five years old. He was caring for me in my mother's absence, and he took me to a liquor store to get himself something to drink. When we got there, he said, "Now, if you just sit in the car and behave yourself, I'll buy you some chips and a soda."

Those were special treats for me, so I promised to sit there, patiently waiting for him to return. As I recall this memory, I remember my feet barely hung over the edge of the car seat, so I had to be very young at the time.

I wanted to earn his acceptance and love. When Ma worked a first-shift job, he worked a second-shift one. One day as he was getting ready for work, I was in the kitchen preparing sandwiches for him. I made perhaps ten sandwiches. I rationalized that if I, as a kid, could eat half of a sandwich, he would eat much more. This memory makes me smile because I remember my parents laughing and Ma thanking me for trying to help. Daddy rarely acknowledged my efforts, but I did what I could to open that door.

The older I got, the more embarrassed I became with his drinking and the way he acted in general. I stopped laughing at him when I realized that his behavior was induced by alcohol and that he was choosing to serve that habit, rather than to be a part of my life.

When I was in middle school, my mother returned to school herself to become a licensed practical nurse. Daddy worked at a tanning factory operating a machine that turned cowhide into leather. He always worked evenings, while Ma worked various shifts. He would get off work around eleven o'clock in the evening but wouldn't arrive home until hours later. Daddy would often visit bars and hang out with his friends and coworkers.

Eventually I accepted that Daddy and I would not have a relationship. After all, when I wanted to be acknowledged and noticed by him and received nothing but silence in return, I judged that his actions spoke volumes about how little he valued me. It's a lesson I had to learn the hard way several times as a child.

Growing up, I felt women ruled the world. They were leaders. They earned a living. Women made the decisions. They kept the family intact and functioning. Men, sad to say, simply helped to procreate children and were not nurturing.

It was not at all the ideal foundation upon which a young girl could build a successful life.

Lesson Learned: No Matter the Early Messages Received, the Truth Is I Had Been Created in Love.

Regardless of what was spoken of me in my mother's womb, as a child, or even as an adult, the truth is I was created in love. My heavenly Father knew what challenges my family would have, and purposed me to be a part of them. I must incorporate forgiveness into my daily life. As painful memories of the past enter my thoughts, I deliberately choose to subject those thoughts to God's word. If it doesn't align with His truth, I must renounce it. Forgiveness doesn't mean that I pretend traumatic events didn't occur; rather, I decide to forgive (others or myself) to continue walking in God's love. For love covers a multitude of sins and certainly covers mine and my parents' sins (see 1 Pet. 4:8).

Photo 1: A joyful memory of picture day at school as a child

CHAPTER 2

A Broken Foundation

Therefore whoever hears these sayings of Mine, and does them, I will liken him to a wise man who built his house on the rock: and the rain descended, the floods came, and the winds blew and beat on that house; and it did not fall, for it was founded on the rock. But everyone who hears these sayings of Mine, and does not do them, will be like a foolish man who built his house on the sand: and the rain descended, the floods came, and the winds blew and beat on that house; and it fell. And great was its fall.

—Matt. 7:24–27

I remember having a relatively close relationship with Grandmo. She was a kind and caring woman who supported me, although I wouldn't describe her as being nurturing.

She led a very hard life and died prematurely in her early sixties. Grandmo went undiagnosed with diabetes for years before her health began to decline. She would eventually require amputation of both legs and an arm when she was in her fifties. I learned later that Grandmo attempted to take her own life after becoming a triple amputee. It was an unsuccessful attempt, but it seemed that she had given up on her life. She was never the same person after that.

When Grandmo was confined to a wheelchair, she went to stay

with my aunt Cecilia, where she could live in a first-floor bedroom. Our entire family would frequently visit her in the evenings and on weekends. Many people saw Grandmo as a pillar in the family. I do recall her sisters visiting during the summers and Grandmo helping family members who were in some sort of crisis.

I spent a lot of time with Grandmo as a young child. She frequently cared for me when Ma was working. She was a respected authority figure in my life and would make meals for me, my siblings, and my cousins. She'd also make desserts that I absolutely loved. Unfortunately, I don't recall her ever cradling me and assuring me that everything would be okay. My fondest memories of being with her were taking trips to the local bakery.

I later learned Grandmo had scolded Ma for the way she treated my father before I was born. She would admonish Ma to leave him alone if she truly wasn't interested. He likely had more affection for Ma than she had for him. I imagine he pulled back to protect his own heart. I would learn later that he didn't follow through on marrying Ma because he suspected Patrick was still in the picture.

By the time I was ten years old, Grandmo was in no position to care for me anymore. I was a latchkey kid. I was often left in charge of my younger brother, Tommy, and younger cousin Lonnie until Ma would come home from work. While Ma was at work, Grandmo would call to check in on us. As soon as I demonstrated that I could wash dishes and cook a meal, I was allowed to make a snack for us before dinner.

Grandmo grew up in Mississippi. I don't know much about her life as a little girl. I was told stories about how she met the man who would become my grandfather. He had a reputation in the community and, as a confident ladies' man, he could likely have had his pick of several women. I don't know how long Grandmo and Mr. Wilder dated, but he emotionally detached from the relationship much sooner than she did. His name was Oscar, but I called him Mr. Wilder because I never really knew him. I remember seeing him once when he was in the hospital, yet I was a young child at the time.

Mr. Wilder broke my grandmother's heart by marrying another woman. He had several children with his wife, and h e built his life around her. Grandmo didn't want life to pass her by, so she moved on and married another man. They had one daughter, my oldest aunt Fannie Mae, but Grandmo's heart was always with Mr. Wilder.

When Mr. Wilder's wife died, my grandmother packed up Fannie Mae and took her to my great grandmother's house. She explained to my aunt that she was going to go down the road to look after Mr. Wilder and his children. The shift in her household devastated Fannie Mae. She cried for months knowing that her mother had left her to care for another family. Grandmo was on a mission to prove to Mr. Wilder that she was the woman he should have chosen the first time around. Unfortunately, in doing so, she subjected herself to a tremendous amount of verbal and, eventually, physical abuse by Mr. Wilder.

Mr. Wilder's children from his first wife were either in high school or already working when their mother died. Grandmo would eventually divorce her first husband and have three daughters with Mr. Wilder, including Ma. When my youngest aunt, Katie, was born, Mr. Wilder opted to relocate to the Midwest where well-paying factory jobs were plentiful at the time.

Grandmo was reluctant to leave her mother and Fannie Mae, as well as her support system in Mississippi. Mr. Wilder took Ma to Milwaukee with him while Grandmo remained behind with Katie.

Ma, being five years old at the time, was so afraid that she wouldn't stop crying. Mr. Wilder called Grandmo to plead with her to come to Wisconsin, as he didn't know how to console Ma.

Fannie Mae had graduated from high school and maintained a

desire to live near Grandmo. She followed Grandmo to Wisconsin and soon found a job in Milwaukee. When Grandmo moved to Wisconsin with Mr. Wilder, Ma became distressed.

Ma told stories of violent arguments between Grandmo and Mr. Wilder to the point that my young mother had to duck to avoid being hit by knives being thrown between the two adults. I believe these events caused Ma to not want a relationship with my grandfather.

Eventually Grandmo grew tired of the abuse and turned to a church for help, as she was now a single parent raising her youngest two girls on her own. She became a nanny for a wealthy Caucasian couple. During that time of Grandmo working, less time was spent with Ma and Katie. I guess that meant that they, too, were latchkey kids and would have to fend for themselves until Grandmo returned home.

In her newfound freedom from Mr. Wilder, Grandmo started dating other men, which required Ma to share what little attention she enjoyed from her mother with Grandmo's suitors. Unfortunately, abuse would now pass on to Grandmo's daughters during this time.

There was a lack of healthy nurturing for Ma when she was a child. She did her best to build a family upon the broken foundation of her own life.

What both Ma and Grandmo needed was a kind, supportive father who would love them unconditionally. That kind of love could only be found in their heavenly Father. I believe their perception of men would have been very different had there been a true understanding of the father's role and God's role in their lives.

Lesson Learned: Sin Blinds Us from Seeing the Truth and Walking in Love.

My grandmother, mother, and I are three generations of women who had a divine purpose before we were conceived. We were called to be children of God through Christ Jesus, and are to love one another (see Eph. 1:3, 5, 18; 1 John 3:23).

To have a correct understanding of a father's love, I had to look at God, who is love. I began to understand His love by meditating on what it means to be adopted and called as a child of God. I suspect my grandfather didn't know how to demonstrate true love of a husband or father, because he lacked the example in his life. Through prayer, I've gone before the Lord to repent of the sins of fathers in my family and to release forgiveness for their shortcomings. Jesus set the example of forgiveness whereby a sinful woman could show great love in washing His feet with her tears and hair and by anointing Him with oil (see Luke 7:36–48). Likewise, I have forgiven Grandmo, Ma, and myself for the choices made related to men in our lives that has led to trauma. This important step unlocked the spiritual blessings God has for me, and it allowed me to walk in love.

Photo 2: Sitting in the hand emerging from the ground at a park in DC as a teenager

CHAPTER 3

Seeking a Father

He will also go before Him in the spirit and power of Elijah, to turn the hearts of the fathers to the children, and the disobedient to the wisdom of the just, to make ready a people prepared for the Lord.

—*Luke 1:17*

I was seven years old when I started to feel a longing in my heart to know who my father was. I believe that is the age when most children begin to understand the role of a mother and father, and they desire a close relationship with both. At that age, they can certainly discern the absence of one or the other from their lives. That's about the time that my sister, Rose, met her father.

My neighborhood consisted of working-class families with mostly married couples and some single mothers raising their kids. It was permissible to simply know that I had a father and knew his name, even if I never got to spend time with him. For me and my sister, it was a big deal to meet our fathers for the first time.

I know my sister was super excited to meet her father. We were both old enough to understand that Daddy was not our real father. Ma was very forthright in telling us that.

I remember we were sitting around the kitchen table one morning when Ma announced that Rose would meet her father that day. My sister was eleven years old at the time, and I was just eight. Rose was painfully shy, but I was the opposite. I was bold, confident, and willing to talk to anybody. I had no fear.

By this time, Rose's father, Stephen, was in his late twenties and owned a tavern about 20 minutes from the neighborhood where we grew up. Ma packed both of us in the car and drove us to the tavern. She stayed in the car and allowed me to make the introduction. Mind you, I had never met my sister's father before. Years later, Rose told me the reason why Ma didn't want to go inside the tavern to see Stephen was due to a long-standing offense she had against him.

It must have been relatively early in the day when we arrived because I remember there was a lot of sunlight coming into the building. I walked in the door with my sister at my side, and loudly announced, "We're here to see Stephen. Is Stephen here?"

The man behind the bar raised his hand and, with a proud look, replied, "That would be me."

I gently pushed my sister on her back and loudly proclaimed, "Rose, go meet your daddy," and watched her walk to the bar.

Stephen poured me a soda and served it to me at a nearby table as Rose crawled onto what I considered to be a huge bar-stool. I sipped my soda slowly while listening to pieces of their conversation as they made small talk. He asked Rose questions about her hobbies, how she liked school, and what her favorite things to do were.

There was one other man in the tavern, and he engaged me with some questions from time to time as my sister talked to her father. When I finished my soda, I left to join Ma in the car, and we sat together for almost 30 minutes before Rose returned. Ma never did go inside.

Rose was exuberant when she emerged and more confident than I had ever recalled seeing her. She was glowing with happiness, as though she had found a missing piece to her puzzle. In reality, she had.

I longed to enjoy that same experience myself and began to imagine the day I would eventually be allowed to meet my father.

For days after meeting her father, Rose would recall tidbits of what they had talked about. One morning during breakfast, I proclaimed that I, too, would have a similar conversation with my father when it was my turn.

But Rose stunned me with the announcement, "Well, you're not going to do that, because your daddy died in Vietnam."

I could feel the life slipping out of me as tears welled in my eyes in stunned disbelief. I can't recall what Ma was doing at the time, but she was nearby and overheard my sister's comment to me. All she did was chastise Rose by saying, "You shouldn't tell your sister that."

She neither confirmed nor denied that my father was dead. Yet I was left with the impression that I would never meet my father, because he had died in the war.

After the initial introduction, Rose was able to forge a relationship not only with Stephen but also with his entire family. She continued her relationship with him until he died when she was nearly thirty years old.

Over time, I learned there were some other family connections to Stephen. He had an aunt whose daughter was one of Rose's paternal cousins. She lived in a large home with her grandparents in Milwaukee.

It was interesting to see how they all related to one another on a personal level. In fact, I was a bit jealous of the relationships because I had absolutely no connection to my father's side of the family— not an aunt, not a cousin, not even a friend of a friend.

I was in junior high school before I learned that my father did not die in Vietnam, and that he was very much alive. But I was forbidden from attempting to contact him. I was told Daddy would be the only father figure I would ever know, and it felt like a punishment to me.

To this day, Ma will not have a conversation with me about my father, Randolph. According to her, they met, she became pregnant with me, and he refused to pay child support. Ma says that he slandered her name. As hurtful as this may seem, I don't think it's a valid reason to keep me from developing a relationship with him. Why should I be punished for the sins of my father?

Ma and Daddy had dated for a while before breaking up and before he was sent to Vietnam in the final years of the war. Ma was renting an apartment in a duplex. She would leave Rose in Grandmo's care and would occasionally go out to tavern parties on the weekends. My parents met at one of those parties and became a couple who spent a lot of time together.

Randolph would hang out with members of my mother's family, and he soon became embroiled in some family dynamics. Their relationship ended before Ma learned she was pregnant with me.

Ma never talked about my father, even casually, and for me to even bring him up was strongly discouraged. I was finally given a few photos of Randolph. At least I could put a face to his name. I studied the features of my father and decided that I bore many of his facial characteristics.

It would be many years before I would ever be able to meet my father, but the desire burned deep in my heart. That desire for a genuine father-daughter relationship was fanned after I encountered a special family during my second year of college.

Lesson Learned: It Is God's Design for Us to Have Spiritual Covering.

In Genesis 3, Eve was deceived by the serpent and took a bite out of the fruit. She allowed the cunning voice of the serpent to trick her into believing that she would not truly die by eating from the Tree of Knowledge. She believed Satan and succumbed to that lie. In the process, she convinced her husband, who perhaps was nearby, that he should sin as well. Adam was created first, and God gave His instructions to Adam who, in turn, gave the instructions to Eve. Regardless, they both knew what God expected of them in the Garden of Eden. Eve was to be covered or protected by Adam as her husband.

As a single woman, God is my covering. This protective covering has benefits, because the Lord will bring me back to Him, even when I stray. For He has placed a desire in my heart to know Him and His ways (see Jer. 24:6–8).

With that being said, there are people in my life for whose well-being I am responsible. It might be an employee; it might be a family member or a very good friend. As a leader, I bear the responsibility of providing a spiritual covering for those I serve.

Photo 3: Picture taken of me after a day hike in the Georgia Appalachian Mountains

CHAPTER 4

Early Influencers

Only take heed to yourself, and diligently keep yourself, lest you forget the things your eyes have seen, and lest they depart from your heart all the days of your life. And teach them to your children and your grandchildren.

—*Deut. 4:9*

I really didn't have any father figures growing up, but women like Ma, Grandmo, and maternal aunts had a great deal of influence on my early life. As I got older, I became interested in families that didn't look like mine, and I'd silently study them.

Brenda was one of my best friends from grade school. After her mother passed away, Brenda and her brother were raised by their aunt and her husband. He was a very peaceful man, and Brenda really loved him. He was quiet, kind, and caring. I had a lot of respect for him because nothing ever seemed to upset him.

Another friend from my early years, Doreen, was a PK (a preacher's kid). I don't remember too much about her father either. He didn't seem to be a nurturing kind of man, but he was involved in Doreen's life, and she respected him.

When I was in fourth grade, Ma enrolled me in a Catholic school that was in our neighborhood. I attended class there until I went to high school. The priests were the only real male figures and I would see them throughout the week, especially during mass.

For many years, Ma would take us to mass, but then she sort of pulled away. I'm not sure what motivated her to make the switch, but she stopped going to church. I felt God might be the answer to what was missing in my life, but I certainly didn't feel I deserved a relationship with Him.

I didn't quite understand His role or see how God fit into the overall scope of my life. Yet knowing that I had a heavenly Father was better than having no father at all.

I applied many of the same traits to God that I applied to Daddy. I thought God was distant and pretty much unapproachable. I considered Him to be very holy. Unfortunately, I believed I wasn't worthy of an intimate relationship with the triune God—God the Father, God the Son, and God the Holy Spirit.

I blamed God for allowing me to grow up without a father and in an environment that wasn't entirely supportive of me as a person. Looking back, He protected me during those years and provided everything I needed, even though I didn't see His role at the time.

I heard messages at church about an all-powerful, all-knowing God, and I was told He cared about all people, including me.

My social activities and school functions filled a deep need for me to interact with others. Even though I would not have considered myself to be athletic by any stretch of the imagination, I joined every sports team the school offered just so that I could belong to a group.

Being involved in sports and school groups gave me the excuse I needed to avoid having to be at home. It helped that the school was in my neighborhood, and if I told Ma where I was, she didn't object to me being there as often as I was.

While growing up in Milwaukee in the 1970s, it was still acceptable and even expected that children would play outside. We had a television, and as kids, we mainly watched cartoons and the

Afterschool Specials on ABC. I do remember the Afterschool Specials. Each had a moral lesson of some sort that would speak to something I related to at home, in my neighborhood, or at school.

People in the neighborhood sort of looked out for one another, so I felt very safe riding my bicycle or playing with friends. Jumping rope was a big thing for me, and I became very good at Double Dutch. Each girl had to have great timing and coordination to jump rope to a rhythm without getting tangled. My friends and I could jump rope for hours.

The rule was that I could go pretty much anywhere in the neighborhood for about a mile in any direction from my house, and I could stay out all day long in the summertime. When the street lights came on, that was my signal that I needed to be home.

One of the girls I liked to hang out with during those years was Sara. She was the only girl in a house full of brothers—good-looking brothers I might add. Sara and I were on the basketball team in junior high school, and her father was the coach. He was a nice man and very patient with us as we played basketball.

─ Starting My Own Path ─

It wasn't until I got into high school that I met someone who I considered to be a good father. My friend Cassandra was a "daddy's girl" and just relished her father's attention. She was raised by her father after her parents divorced. He was a lot of fun, and he really treated me well.

Cassandra's father made it his mission to make me laugh every time I saw him. Maybe he saw a void in my life and wanted to fill it. He was a hands-on type of father who was very involved in Cassandra's life. He was also very affectionate, hugging or kissing her or even just putting his arm around her. He treated her like a little princess, and that's the type of father I always wanted. I thought Cassandra had the coolest father in the world, and I enjoyed hanging out at her house in order to be around them. He really stood out as being unique, and I remember Cassandra having a great deal of confidence growing up.

In my family, if fathers played a role in their children's lives at all, it was a distant one. I decided when I would have children, I wanted my husband to be like Cassandra's father.

Cassandra and my other friend Linda were my closest friends in high school. We were always hanging out together. We looked so much alike that we told ourselves that we were somehow related. Their mothers treated me like a daughter, and Ma really liked Cassandra and Linda too.

Even throughout college, the three of us tried to stay in touch while attending different schools. Today, we're still good friends. It's not often that we're all together in the same place, but when we are, it's like we can pick up right where we left off as if we just saw each other the day before. We're each pouring into one another's lives, happy and rejoicing in good times or offering a listening ear and shoulder to cry on in difficult times.

I was also really close to my sister, Rose, when we were growing up. She was the ideal big sister. She protected me, and I looked up to her. Best of all, she would let me hang out with her friends, and that was a big deal for me. I liked being around older people. I don't know why, but I felt more mature and grown up just being with them.

When I was in junior high, Rose and her friends would take me to concerts or teenage parties, but they never encouraged me to do things that would be bad for me. Hanging out with them also gave me a lot of clout with kids my age because I got to enjoy many things they didn't get to do.

By the time I got to high school, I had my own little social circle, and I spent a lot of time with them. I think being with Rose and her friends gave me a lot of confidence, because I was rather outgoing in high school. The social aspect of high school was very fulfilling for me. I really needed that social outlet as a way to escape from all the confusion happening in my home and family relationships.

My friends became more like a family to me. I knew my family was pretty dysfunctional, but my friends filled the void. I started to believe that not everybody's family functioned like mine. Being with my friends made me feel supported, affirmed, encouraged, and loved. I very much liked operating in that type of social circle.

At some point, Rose was hoping I'd return the favor and invite her to hang out with my friends. I suspect the close "family" relationships we had, as well as the fun activities we were doing together, really appealed to her.

Unfortunately, I didn't pick up on her suggestions. It didn't occur to me that she would even want to associate with a group of younger girls. Hanging out with her little sister was one thing, but Rose wanting to spend time with a whole group of younger teens didn't make sense to me. I realized the oversight after it was too late to do anything about it.

I had moved out of state to attend college, and Rose stayed behind to deal with the family drama. Once I left Milwaukee, I developed a new life and a support system that was separate from Rose and the rest of my family.

— A Loving Family —

At Hampton University, I had the opportunity to get to know more men. One of my favorite teachers was Reverend Langford. He was my biology teacher, and I really came to admire him. He was tremendously influential in my life by fanning my enthusiasm for school and interest in biology.

One day Reverend Langford invited me to his home to enjoy dinner with his family. That was my first real experience watching a healthy family dynamic. Reverend Langford was married and had two daughters. I admired the nurturing relationship his girls had with him, and the loving relationship Reverend Langford had with his wife. They freely hugged and kissed each other, which fascinated me. His daughters felt comfortable enough to sit on his lap and lean back to rest on his chest.

They would talk excitedly about something and say things, for example, "Oh, Daddy, guess what I did today?" and he would respond, encouraging his girls to share whatever they wanted as he attentively listened. I had only seen family relationships like that on television. My experience in Reverend Langford's home opened my eyes to show me that children really could have loving, supportive, and nurturing relationships with their fathers, and fathers could be actively involved in the day-to-day lives of their children.

Deep in my heart, I longed for that type of fatherly relationship. The love expressed in that home was evident, and a peace permeated that environment. I felt very comfortable there and am grateful they welcomed me into their home.

I don't know if I'd go as far as to say that Reverend Langford was my first father figure, because I didn't dare sit in his lap or engage him in any type of physical affection. But I grew to really appreciate him as a man and as a mentor.

I would often seek advice from him, which he willingly offered. Before I graduated, I did tell him how much I appreciated all he did for me by making me feel so welcome. Still, if I had an important decision to make and wanted a father's input, I did not turn to Reverend Langford. He was always supportive of anything I decided to do. But something in my heart still kept me from putting too much trust in men.

I lost contact with Reverend Langford, but he will always occupy a special place in my heart for opening my eyes to knowing that a genuine, loving family relationship is possible even for me.

As it turned out, I would begin pursuing my Father's love from lost and broken men instead of finding what I truly needed from God.

Lesson Learned: It Is Okay to Cry Out to God, Especially in Anger or Pain.

When bad things happen to us, we can internalize it, dwell upon the situation, and allow it to steal our joy. Or we can be open and honest with God and seek His help.

I like journaling for that reason. I can be as transparent as I need to be, then wait and listen for God's voice. This intimate communication I have with the Father is certainly something I want to share with my family and those of you who may be seeking a way to safely share your thoughts and emotions.

When I was going through a particularly painful journey in my life, I wrote the following in my journal:

> *Lord, I thank you for another day and for the privilege to call upon You. Continue to teach me how to trust You by loving and forgiving others, fearing not, and surrendering control of my life. I love you, Lord, so much. All I need is You.*
>
> *Even when I was in the Army, I remember feeling completely rejected and outcast by so many, and You were my only comfort.*
>
> *I never felt that I measured up in the Army. I know I began to withdraw and feel like I was in some sort of prison. I tried to meet that basic need for acceptance by obtaining love through intimate relationships. Lord, it was You showing me that I was trying to meet my need my way, not Your way.*
>
> *Lord, I thank You for loving me enough to show me how hasty my decisions had been in relationships and that You wanted to fill that void. When You spoke to me in 1994, my heart was so comforted. I thank You for that.*

Well, Lord, I'm feeling rejected again by those in my close intimate circle. The difference is that I have the truth. The truth is that You love me and fully accept me. You will not allow the enemy to overtake me.

The individuals involved in this recent situation are not my enemy. Spiritual wickedness is. I have direct access to you, Father, through my prayer life. I have dominion over sin. Lord, I believe You can resolve any problem that appears to be ugly.

Jeremiah 17:7–8 says, "Blessed is the man who trusts in the Lord and whose hope is the Lord, for he shall be a tree planted by the waters which spreads out its roots by the river and will not fear when heat comes, but its leaf will be green and will not be anxious in the year of drought, nor will cease from yielding fruit."

Lord, You know sometimes when I anticipate a situation getting worse, then fear enters the picture. You have said 'the leaf will be green'. That means You will continue to provide the nourishment needed for my survival even when the heat is turned up!

Lord, I am that tree receiving nourishment from You. Despite how things look I know, Lord, that I can trust You to not allow me to be harmed. I keep my focus on You, so that I may bear the fruit of Your Holy Spirit that the world may see You through me.

You truly are my hope. I know that You are in the business of restoration. Lord, show me how not to withdraw from people, but also show me how not to seek the opinions of others. Deal with me on this issue of feeling used.

I rejoice as I look back on this period when I wrote the above prayer, and see the faithfulness of the Father. He brought me through victoriously as my Protector and Restorer. Today, I have meaningful friendships with people I served alongside in the military. Furthermore, God has redeemed me from the mistakes I've made in past romantic relationships.

CHAPTER 5

Meeting Sam

When wisdom enters your heart, and knowledge is pleasant to your soul, discretion will preserve you; understanding will keep you, to deliver you from the way of evil, from the man who speaks perverse things, from those who leave the paths of uprightness to walk in the ways of darkness

— *Prov. 2:10–13*

One of the first serious romantic relationships I had was with a man named Sam. I met him when I was nineteen years old and was just finishing up high school before starting classes at the University of Wisconsin—Whitewater.

Sam was from Tennessee, and he had never lived anywhere else except for a brief stint in Mississippi. He was a professional boxer when I met him, which added a sense of allure to the relationship. He was like a celebrity figure in the boxing world, at least in my mind.

He had just finished a boxing match when I met him at a nightclub. Yes, I was underage; I needed to be twenty-one to enter a nightclub in Wisconsin at that time. But I had an Upward Bound identification card for my college preparatory classes, and no one checking IDs had any idea what Upward Bound was. It sounded legitimate and made me appear older than I was.

Sam and I talked for a bit and really made a connection. He was twenty-five years old at the time. Before the night was over, we exchanged contact information. I could tell he was a "ladies' man," but it didn't bother me. He seemed outgoing and exciting to me. I thought he really lived a life of fame and adventure. After all, he participated in boxing matches throughout the states and overseas.

He was five and a half years older than me, and I thought I had really arrived on the social scene to be in his company. Dating an older man made me feel mature and secure. Until then, I still didn't consider myself to be an adult. But Sam changed that.

He prided himself on his ability to conquer women. It was a real ego boost for him to be able to cite the number of women he had dated.

He was a master manipulator. A chronic liar too. He didn't like to communicate much, but I was intrigued by his silence. It made him more mysterious and attractive to me. Little did I know that it was all part of his deceptive plan to use silence and lies to manipulate me.

I quickly fell in love with Sam. Even though he lived in Tennessee, we carried on a long-distance relationship for more than a year. I could have easily sidetracked my life and wandered off with him. Fortunately, I was intensely focused on starting a career by finishing my college prep courses and applying to various universities.

Thank God I had the advisors I did who kept me focused on pursuing a career, rather than a relationship. No matter how foolish I may have been at that age, it had been drilled into me that I needed to establish the groundwork for a career. I maintained a pretty level head regarding my career goals, but I was still a bit naive with men.

I met Sam in the spring and knew I would be going off to basic training in the Army later that summer. Cell phones back then weren't common and email hadn't even been invented, so I would write a lot of letters to him. Ma certainly wasn't going to pay long-distance telephone charges for me to carry on a relationship with some out-of-state boxer. So I invested in a lot of stamps and stationery. Once Sam would receive one of my letters, he would often respond by calling me later. When he called, Sam turned on the charm. He'd tell me, "Oh,

Terrina, you're the lady of my dreams. You're the type of woman a man like me just has to marry."

Naturally, I read into that tone that he really was moving us down the road toward marriage. But he didn't send me a single letter when I was in basic training. That should have been a red flag. I later learned that although I was dating him exclusively, Sam was not doing the same with me.

As a soldier far from home undergoing a grueling eight-week basic training regiment, mail call was one of the huge highlights of any day. All of the other women in my platoon were getting mail from family members and the guys they were dating. Day after day I was devastated that Sam didn't think enough of me to send even a postcard. Still, I was in love with him.

I would continue to write letters to him, and upon occasion, I would call him by phone when I had some free time. I'd criticize him for not writing to me and tell him how much I would love to receive a letter.

He'd reply, "Terrina, I'm so sorry. I'm just not much of a writer." He was full of excuses. I believe I didn't end the relationship, because I thought it was better to be in one than not.

I finally completed basic training and headed back to Wisconsin for a while before heading off to college. We picked up the phone calls, and I would often hear how much he loved me and how I was the type of woman he would consider marrying.

Sam routinely lured me into forgiving him, and he'd do or say enough that he would remain in my good graces.

Something inside of me was whispering to guard my heart, but my mind was manipulated by his charm and promises. I took what little money I had made during basic training and paid for a bus ticket to visit him.

He didn't have a telephone at home, so there was really no way I could contact him outside of writing a letter. So I sent him a letter revealing my travel plans and telling him the day and time my bus would arrive. There was a little confusion, but he did manage to pick me up on time from the Greyhound station.

One night, he took me to a nightclub, and I met those he socialized with regularly. I was surprised my Upward Bound ID still worked to get me into Tennessee nightclubs. While we were at the nightclub, I sensed a woman in the room was giving me the *stink eye*. Several other people were looking in our direction and talking about us too. I just assumed it was due to Sam being well-known in his small town. When a slow song played, he led me to the dance floor and snuggled close to me.

I was head-over-heels in love with that man—my future husband. But when I reached up and gave him a peck on the cheek, he told me I shouldn't do that, because it would get him in trouble. I was confused and asked him what he meant by that statement, but all he did was chuckle.

Sam was involved with another woman in Tennessee, and it could have been one of the women who had been staring at us. I was devastated and badly hurt. I had just spent my very hard-earned money to visit a cheater. I wanted to leave, but I was stuck.

I didn't have a phone, so I couldn't call a cab even if I wanted to. Besides, where would I go if I left? I was stuck with Sam for transportation and lodging. I spent the rest of the night miserable and wondering how I could have allowed myself to be so easily duped. When we finally left to go back to his house, I was in a foul mood.

One of his friends was driving us around town, which was very odd considering the driver was married himself with a small child. I thought, *What was he doing hanging around with two single people and taking them to a nightclub?*

Later I discovered that Sam was an alcoholic. This friend was trying to stop Sam from damaging yet another vehicle or possibly harming us while driving drunk. Sam's inebriated state seemed normal to me because most men in my life were heavy drinkers. Eventually the friend dropped us off at Sam's house.

The next day, I was ready to head back to the bus station because I had a return ticket to Milwaukee. After Sam sobered up a bit, he was apologetic and returned to his charming character. He even tried to kiss me. It worked to some degree, because my heart softened a bit toward him.

The rest of the day was pretty low-key. He introduced me to some of his relatives, and I watched him play a pickup game of basketball with his friends. Sam's cousins and I sat on his car surrounding the court and watched the game. I wasn't all that interested in sports but went to appease him.

Heading home on the Greyhound bus, I sensed continuing the relationship could be a mistake. I had been so gullible, but I was still in love with Sam. I couldn't reconcile my heart and my mind to accept that the relationship was going nowhere.

When I returned to Milwaukee, I tried forcing myself to not accept his calls. Still, his calls would sometimes catch me off-guard when I'd answer the phone myself.

Knowing how hurt I was that he didn't write to me during basic training, Sam had an opportunity to prove himself again, as I was about to do more Army training (AIT). He tried to write to me, but this time my heart was a little guarded.

Eventually I headed off to college where I met new people and had a few relationships. I really wanted to put Sam behind me, especially when it took him six months to call me. Deep in my heart, I remained in love with him for two more years.

I was still looking for a man or a father figure I could rely upon for love, advice, and support. Yet I was still involved in some unhealthy relationships with my family and friends. Unhealthy in that I had allowed people to define who I was and to determine what were or were not valid feelings. I was consumed with being a people pleaser and didn't understand my own self-worth. It was important to me that I was perceived as normal.

Little did I know how God was already at work orchestrating the next steps in my life that would eventually lead me directly to Him.

Lesson Learned: Healthy Boundaries Are Key to Developing a Healthy Self-image.

If I could just get my college degree, land jobs that would set me on an upward path of success, and have a man to share my life with, I will have true happiness. This was an internal message I frequently played in my mind.

Academic and professional training were methodical and made sense to me. Teachers or supervisors used agendas with clearly defined topics listing goals and objectives. My performance was rated based on a grading scale, which allowed me to advance to the next level in school or my career. Being accomplished or obtaining goals was essential to my identity at that time.

Basically I tried to apply this same approach to my personal life. Sam represented the familiar—a lively, outgoing man with a drinking problem. The grading scale for my personal life was the appearance or absence of a relationship. If I had a relationship, whether healthy or not, meant I had something worth having. I tolerated maltreatment because I thought that's all I deserved. I had to learn my feelings really did matter.

This process would ultimately lead me on a path to forgiving others and putting healthy boundaries in place for my relationships. Acknowledging how Sam, Ma, and others made me feel was initially difficult. I could no longer allow unhealthy relationships to just manifest and wreak havoc in my life.

Gratefully I have had the help of loving friends, ministers, and counselors who have helped me develop boundaries with bothersome traits in others while continuing to be me. In a respectful way, I address issues with people directly without getting angry. If I'm feeling too angry to address a person, I ask God to help me understand the anger and to remove it from my heart.

Apart from Him, I can neither bear the fruit of forgiveness in these relationships nor have the wisdom to end them. I value who I am as a person in all the roles I assume in this life. It is important that I surround myself with people who support my values and my personal boundaries. By this, I can have true fulfillment and experience wholeness daily.

Photo 4: High School cap and gown photo of me

CHAPTER 6

First Encounter with My Father

For every kind of beast and bird, of reptile and creature of the sea, is tamed and has been tamed by mankind. But no man can tame the tongue. It is an unruly evil, full of deadly poison.

— James 3:7–8

I graduated from college in December 1992 and would soon enter the U.S. Army as a second lieutenant.

It was a monumental day when my second lieutenant bars were pinned on me because it was the culmination of my college education, the start of my military career, and a life with my fiancé, Nelson. His parents actually pinned my lieutenant bars on me during the commissioning ceremony.

Because I was now officially entering the military for active duty, I knew I wanted to have detailed information about my medical and family history. I also wanted to be fair to Nelson by disclosing anything that could be passed on to our future children. Avoiding the possibility of marrying a distant cousin was very important to me considering DNA testing wasn't as popular in the 1990s.

Unfortunately, I knew nothing about any hereditary issues on my father's side of the family. I really wanted to know if there were any generational ailments common to the family.

A few weeks after receiving my commission, I came back to Milwaukee. I put Ma on alert that I was going to attempt to contact Randolph while I was home. I visited the county courthouse hoping to find some records based on his name and last known address, but it was a solid roadblock. I couldn't find any information through that channel.

In desperation, I turned to the White Pages, which I should have done years earlier. I started calling all the men who had his last name until I finally connected with him. I introduced myself, and we set a time and place for a meeting, and that was it. We couldn't have talked for more than one minute.

We agreed to meet at a nearby McDonald's because I wanted that first visit to occur in a public place, but he stood me up. Yes, I was very disappointed. It was like being abandoned all over again.

A few days before I was supposed to return to Virginia, I knew I needed to try again. I called and explained that I was leaving soon and that I would come to him. I insisted that he provide me his address and announced I was on my way to his house.

I borrowed Ma's car and drove over to his home. He was living in a tiny boarding house. When I arrived, I was very guarded and prepared for some disappointing words or action on his part.

If I had been given permission to meet my father when I was a child, I would have done so in a heartbeat. I really desired a relationship with him, or at the very least, the opportunity to know more about him. But that was a taboo topic with Ma. It left me with the impression that my father must either be a horrible person or there was some deep, dark secret concerning me that I was never supposed to learn. Overall, I was left to feel that I was the product of my mother's unhappiness.

As an adult, I learned Randolph lived relatively close to us. He, Ma, and Daddy would occasionally see one another at a local bar, which would end in some unpleasant altercation. By never talking about Randolph, I think Ma was trying to shield me from a man she couldn't trust. Still, she let her feelings toward him show at the mention of his name. That did little to diminish my desire to meet him.

—Meeting for the First Time —

I went into that first meeting a few days before Christmas expecting nothing more than honest answers to the few questions I had. I wanted to get inside, get the answers, and get out as quickly as possible. By being emotionally disconnected, I believed I was shielding myself from any form of rejection. Fortunately the encounter didn't pan out as I predicted.

We engaged in conversation, and Randolph was thrilled that I had tried to reach out to him. It was obvious that he really wanted to establish a relationship with me, but I wasn't ready to open my heart to that possibility. The thought that he was absent from my life for so many years made me very suspicious. His excessive drinking would make it very difficult to have a conversation. Alcohol abuse had been a challenge for most men in my family, and it would be a primary reason for division in relationships with my stepfather and father.

Randolph shared countless stories of how he knew of major events in my life, such as graduating from high school, receiving awards, my Army commissioning, and so forth. I was amazed. He had maintained contact with Ma's sisters. They knew where he was all along, but they never let me in on the secret. Ma didn't want anyone speaking of Randolph in her presence. Perhaps my aunts thought they were protecting me and Ma with their silence. I believe the hurt Ma experienced behind the relationship was still very painful and she never managed to forgive him.

I also learned that my cousin Lonnie, who was very much like a brother to me, had dated my half sister, Melinda, while I was away at college. I was surprised. I wondered how he could not tell me about being in a relationship with Melinda knowing she was my sister.

I confronted Lonnie about that relationship years later. He said, "Well, Terri, when she was in my life, you were already off to college and doing your thing. You were long gone when she and I dated."

He swore he didn't know who she was until after they had been dating for a while.

Somehow Lonnie, Melinda, and Randolph all wound up in the same place. When Melinda introduced Lonnie to my father, my father asked simple questions; one being, "Who is your mother?" Lonnie replied that his mother was Katie, to which my father asked if she had a sister named Barbara. When Lonnie replied that she did, my father announced that Barbara gave birth to his daughter, meaning me. Lonnie and Melinda just looked at each other in shock at the revelation.

Lonnie returned home and told his mother what happened. Finally he approached Ma with the news, but she shut him down right away. "I don't want to hear anything about it," she rudely shouted.

There were certain events in her past, especially her relationship with my father, which left her very angry and bitter. Ma would always claim that I could talk to her about absolutely anything, but I knew there were limits to what we could discuss.

Speaking hasty toxic words has caused so much suffering and division in my family that I don't think it was realized until the evidence of hurt became apparent. I believe we must be more careful in how we, as a family, speak to one another.

Randolph and I talked for a while that first time and exchanged telephone numbers. I walked away without feeling that I had finally found "Daddy," and could have a great father-daughter relationship with him. At least I could say I had met him, formed my own opinions about him, and had answers to my basic questions. I was very formal with him and intended to have no further contact with my father after that initial encounter.

There was no way I was going to risk getting close to him only to be rejected later. My mind convinced me that I needed to protect my heart. My reluctance was rooted in a belief that abusive habits with alcohol only caused damage to relationships.

Now, my father began calling me a few months after we met. I had returned to Virginia to pack up my belongings and tie up some loose ends before heading to my first duty station at Fort McClellan, Alabama. Each time he called, he would have flash-backs to some experience in Vietnam. For example, he'd explain that he had just gotten orders to report for duty himself.

I wondered if he was suffering from posttraumatic stress syndrome. I tried to talk him out of whatever he was experiencing in his mind in hopes of bringing him back to reality. He'd call reliving some type of war experience. This happened regularly, and I learned it was something he did to many people who loved him and cared for him.

I suspected Randolph truly loved my mother but struggled with the breakup in the 1970s. He ultimately married a woman who looked similar to Ma. After I got to know his wife, Paula, I realized her story was much like Ma's in that she already had one young child. She was a divorcee when she met Randolph. Once they got married, Randolph accepted her daughter, Renee, as his own. Together they had another daughter, Melinda.

Many years later, Randolph admitted that he was overcome with guilt about raising Renee as his stepdaughter while not having any contact with me, his biological daughter.

Those first encounters in Milwaukee and over the phone in 1992 left me guarded and afraid of pursuing a relationship with Randolph. Based on how distant I was with him, I believe he sensed my hesitation, and chose to shy away.

In 2011, all that changed.

Lesson Learned: Don't Put Too Much Stock in What Others Think or Say.

One of the things God has taught me over the years is that I put too much stock in what people say. I believed them when they either spoke aloud or silently showed their actions that indicated that neither my feelings nor me as a person even mattered to them.

I matter to God, and I will continue to matter, not only while I walk on the face of this earth but also throughout all of eternity. No matter what emotions I may be experiencing, I do matter. Furthermore, I am loved and have a purpose in this life. I really wrestled with believing this truth about God versus believing the lies from Satan, accusing me saying, "No one really cares about you. You're weird. You're strange. You'll never measure up. You just need to stay out of the way because you don't belong. You don't belong in this group or that group."

Those are all lies of the enemy that kept me bound in the mindset of rejection and kept me living in fear of letting my true personality come forth.

That type of bondage crept up on me from the time I was a young girl and followed me even after I became an adult. It stewed and festered inside of me. Yet I learned that I am more than victorious. I am more than a conqueror in Jesus Christ. Because I abide in Him and He abides in me, I can do all things through Him.

Through many prayers, I received the affirmation from God that I had desperately wanted to hear from my parents.

CHAPTER 7

Nelson's Influence and Falter

Do not fear, for you will not be ashamed; neither be disgraced, for you will not be put to shame; for you will forget the shame of your youth, and will not remember the reproach of your widowhood anymore. For your Maker is your husband, the LORD of hosts is His name; and your Redeemer is the Holy One of Israel; He is called the God of the whole earth.

—Isa. 54:4–5

In the fall of 1992, it was a busy time for me, as I was wrapping up my time at Hampton University. I was involved in ROTC and working two part-time jobs to help make ends meet, as money was very tight then. It also appeared more and more likely that my Army Reserve unit would be deployed to the Middle East, so I was also preparing to go to war. I often experienced enormous levels of stress operating on only four hours of sleep daily during that time.

I was living in a boarding house with five other college women, not too far from the campus. My room was a converted greenhouse. There was no insulation, and it was simply attached to the house. It got cold in Virginia, and that room reflected the outdoor temperature. When the sun was out, it would warm up slightly. But at night and during cloudy days, the cold seemed to reach the core of my bones.

Having a landline telephone in our individual rooms was how we handled our calls and maintained the peace in the household. Except there wasn't a telephone jack in this greenhouse room. One of my girlfriends knew a fellow student, Nelson, who knew a handyman who could install a telephone jack in my room.

I called Nelson to see if something could be worked out. I learned the installer was an underemployed guy Nelson knew from his hometown. He would do odd jobs whenever he could just to get by financially. Nelson was trying to help him out by referring people he knew who needed small projects done around their homes.

Nelson served as the intermediary and helped make the appointment. Both came to my room one afternoon to install the telephone jack. I was grateful that Nelson had come along. I wasn't too trusting of the locals, especially if they weren't students. With Nelson being a student, I felt more comfortable having him there.

They had arrived when I was unloading my car and I learned later that Nelson was checking me out as he drove up. He told me that he liked what he saw.

It took quite some time to complete the installation, but Nelson's friend got a phone line working in the greenhouse room. After the installation was done, Nelson's friend wanted to leave, but Nelson was trying to find excuses to remain in conversation with me. I liked the attention he showed me, and he seemed like a "safe" guy. We joked and laughed, but I also tried explaining that I had an incredibly busy schedule.

I finally agreed to meet him again later. He would often bring me prepared meals, which was really a blessing. All six of us women living in the house were responsible for buying our own food and cooking our own meals. It got a little hectic with all of us sharing space in the community kitchen, but we made it work. Best of all, I didn't have to compete for cooking time when Nelson brought home-cooked meals to me.

Because my schedule was so busy and sleep a precious commodity, I often took advantage of any downtime to catch a 30-minute nap. I'd take off my pants, leave my top on, and climb into bed. It was rare for me to have guests. But if my housemates would tell me I had a visitor, I'd scramble to get dressed and greet whoever showed up.

Nelson had this tendency to drop by unannounced. A few times he would stop by when I was in bed watching TV. One of my housemates would let him into the hallway right outside my room. When my name was called from the other side of the door, it would often be Nelson. We would talk for a bit while I was lying in bed. When it was time for him to leave, he would expect me to get out of bed and walk him to the front door.

Embarrassed, I would tell him that he would have to see himself out because I wasn't wearing any pants. He would laugh and agree to leave, but the pattern continued. I guess he saw an impromptu visit with a free meal as a way to get into my good graces. Nelson was my knight in shining armor, coming to rescue me from the stress of college life by injecting a little fun and humor into my daily routine.

Eventually we started spending more time together. I was flattered with all the attention Nelson was showing me. He was enthusiastic and uplifting, which was something I really needed during that stressful period.

By that point, a few years had passed since I had broken up with Sam, and I had dated another man who I considered my best friend at the time, Hector. But I didn't think Hector was interested in any commitments. I had a few little relationships here and there, but nothing serious because my heart was still healing from the disappointment I felt with the ones that failed.

In fact, I wasn't really pursuing any relationships when I met Nelson. I was truly focused on finishing school, starting my career, facing deployment, and conducting military training with my Army Reserve unit. It was important to keep me and my other soldiers alive.

I felt safe around Nelson because he seemed so clean and pure. I wasn't a practicing Christian at the time, but Nelson was, and he professed his belief to me on several occasions. I think that's why I considered him to be a safe guy to allow into my very complicated life.

I allowed Nelson to pursue me, and we dated exclusively for two years.

Nelson majored in architecture, as did several of my friends, so we all enjoyed socializing at local college parties and events. Despite the reservations my friends had about my relationship with Nelson, they never shared their concerns with me at the time, because they could see how happy I was. But I learned later that they considered us a rather odd couple.

Nelson was kind of awkward socially and preferred to spend time with me alone. I, on the hand, was a social butterfly who enjoyed hanging out with people and attending parties. I had been that way since junior high school. I was always comfortable in social settings, but he seemed out of place.

At some point, he started to exert some pressure to persuade me to not hang out with my friends. Eventually it got to be a bit irritating. I wasn't accustomed to a man trying to control whatever I did.

I also made the mistake of asking for his help in keeping me physically fit. Being in the military, it was very important to keep my weight under control—it was critical, as an officer, to be within the weight standards. I was borderline for my age and height.

Every time I took a physical fitness test, my weight was recorded along with the results and they became part of my personnel file. Being overweight or unfit could have jeopardized my career.

My problem was that although I enjoyed working out, I really loved to eat. So I asked him to help me stay in shape and maintain control of my weight. The way he opted to do so was rather insensitive.

He'd see me eating something and ask, "Are you going to eat *that*?"

I'd respond sarcastically, "You see me putting it into my mouth? So, yeah." I just didn't like his approach, and I would see it in a negative light rather than as him trying to remind me I needed to make better choices. He would respond with comments that would just pierce my self-esteem, such as, "I guess you're never going change how you eat."

That really hurt me. Nelson was an only child with control issues, and he had been pampered by his parents. They catered to him in a way that neither I nor any of my friends had experienced. I think that contributed to his mindset.

I remember him describing how his parents had included him in their marriage. It wasn't a ceremony uniting husband and wife, but uniting the three of them. The way he described it, I gathered that their family relationship was such that if his father slacked off in providing emotional support to his mom, then Nelson was expected to fill in the gap.

When she didn't receive the desired support and encouragement from her husband, she would turn to their son. That put a lot of pressure on him to meet her emotional needs when it wasn't his responsibility.

It put a lot of pressure on our relationship too. Nelson would share things with his mother that I shared with him in confidence. He didn't have enough maturity to realize that you just don't talk to your mom about some topics. I thought it was very unusual.

His awkwardness was noticed by our mutual friends too. If there was some injustice at school, we knew how to work within the system to resolve problems. Not Nelson.

In situations that may have been a disappointment to others, for Nelson it became a supreme injustice. He approached it not from a "let's get this problem fixed" mindset, but rather he embraced heightened emotionalism. I knew that getting worked up about a problem wasn't going to settle anything.

Nelson had some anger issues. I remember visiting him one day after work to discover that he had literally punched holes into his wall.

There were also holes in his door and fist prints in the sidewall. He readily admitted that as a young child, his parents had to help him manage his anger in a healthy way.

At Hampton University, one of the traditions that make it such a wonderful small community is that upperclassmen were paired to freshmen as their little brothers or little sisters. It helped the freshmen adapt to college life and ensured that they had an older, wiser mentor to guide them through their first year. It was supposed to be an informal friendship.

For some reason, Nelson had paired himself with a freshman girl, and she became pregnant that year. I don't believe he was the father, but he internalized the pregnancy and got very angry with her when she made her announcement. That's when he punched holes in the walls. I thought that was a little extreme. His response caused me to wonder if there wasn't something more to that relationship than he was letting on.

Living in that little greenhouse room without insulation was also beginning to impact my health. I would often spend more time at Nelson's house during the winter months than I did in my own freezing room.

Eventually I moved out of that house to rent a room in the house of a coworker when I worked for a local hospital. It was there that I met this emergency room nurse, an elderly lady who became my spiritual mom. She was a shining example of what unconditional love looked like.

This precious woman took me into her very modest home and welcomed me into her family. She confided in me that she had been raped in that house. I would later become very uncomfortable being in the home knowing this violation happened to her.

She was a widow who had been living alone for quite a while. Apparently, someone had been stalking and watching her before finally breaking into the home. She woke up in the middle of the night and noticed the silhouette of a person at the end of her bed. As she screamed, he attacked and raped her. The rapist was eventual caught and brought to justice. During the trial he asked her to forgive him which she did. She understood forgiving him would liberate her.

The nurse's family rallied around her and encouraged her to live with them, but she wanted to retain her independence. So they renovated the home and installed security windows and bars. I learned later that the attacker gained access to the house through the window in my room. After she shared that experience with me, I spent even more time with Nelson than I had before.

-Nelson's Falter-

As the summer of 1992 progressed, I stayed in the Hampton Roads area to work. I really needed money at that point. I only had two semesters of college left before I would graduate and enter the Army.

Nelson and I were pretty much inseparable that summer, but I was beginning to feel smothered by his attention. If I wasn't with him at some point every day, it was as though something was wrong. He continued to show up unannounced, regardless of whether I had plans or really needed to focus on my studies. He demanded a lot of my attention.

One evening I heard his little sports car pull into the backyard of the house where I lived. He expected me to drop my plans and go off somewhere with him. I told him I had other plans and that he should have called before driving over to my house. He looked hurt as he watched me and my friends drive off.

I left him standing at the steps as I got into the car with my friends and drove away. My friends were really concerned because they didn't want to come between Nelson and me as a couple. I reassured them we were doing the right thing. Nelson needed to learn that he could not continue to just show up and demand my full attention.

We had a great time, and I guess Nelson just went home and sulked. Later he called and told me that he and his parents had been talking about me, my career, and my decision to join the Army.

Frankly, I was kind of offended by the discussion.

"Oh, really," I said flippantly. "What did the three of you decide?" I wanted him to know that I really didn't care what his parents thought about my career choice. I felt that I had the final say about my life choices, even if it would cause a conflict in our relationship. But I began to sense he and I were not going to make it.

Nelson explained that his father had been drafted and served in Vietnam. Consequently, after having several bad experiences while serving, his father had a huge chip on his shoulder about the military and the Army in particular. Nelson's father didn't desire to have any part of military service, and he really didn't want his son or anyone else he cared for to be connected to the military.

Nelson managed to adopt his father's view of the military and basically told me that if the two of us were going to get married, then I would need to begin planning my exit from the military. I replied bluntly, "Well, that's not going to happen. Next question."

I reminded him that before he ever arrived on the scene and entered my life, this plan was already in the making. I had no intention of forgoing all my plans for a career just because he, and especially his father, didn't like the military. I was very angry at the suggestion.

Nelson got quiet and then started to cry. "Well, I guess this means our relationship is ending," he said.

I asked why it would have to end just because I was serving in the Army. But I also told him that if he truly felt that strongly about it, then I was willing to accept his decision and our relationship would, in fact, end.

Then he had a change of heart. "Terrina, let's try to make the best of it. Maybe something will change."

I interpreted that to mean that maybe I would change my mind, come to my senses, and comply with his family's desire that I not seek a career in the military. Ironically my military career would only last six years.

We continued to see each other after that, but the relationship was severely strained. Eventually I graduated, and within two months, I was to report to Fort Campbell, Kentucky.

That was like an "ahh-ha" moment for Nelson. He realized it was a new day and a new era. People were no longer drafted into the Army just to go to war. It really could be a career. In fact, the first Gulf War had already ended, and America was experiencing an uneasy peace. During this time, Nelson had another semester to complete before graduating.

We had a heart-to-heart talk about the realities of military life for the military spouse of an Army officer. "Now, listen. If we're going to move forward in our relationship, then you need to understand that I will be an Army officer, and you're a civilian. That means I outrank you," I said.

I explained that when we attended military functions together, I would be introduced first, followed by him. We would be presented to others as Lieutenant Wilder and her guest, Nelson. That was all part of military protocol. I needed him to understand that and be willing to accept it.

He assured me that he was okay with that. "I'm very confident in who I am, so I don't need any etiquette or rules to dictate who I am as a man," he explained.

I told him to keep that in mind, because if we married, things wouldn't change. I asked him specifically if he understood. "I know you grew up knowing that the man is the head of the household, but as far as military etiquette is concerned, rank comes first. Can you deal with that?"

He replied that the military couldn't dictate what would happen in our home, and he was right. Still, he assured me that he understood and that he could live in that type of social environment. I had my doubts due to his father's enlisted experience, but officers followed a different set of rules.

We later attended a military ball, and Nelson was incredibly awkward. He held up well, even though he wanted me by his side the entire time. I think he felt out of place. While I was expected to mingle with all the other attendees, Nelson really wanted to just sit off to the side. Eventually I had to leave him sitting at a table in order to fulfill my obligation.

We were growing apart in many ways, even among our other interests. My life was intensifying, and he really hadn't set any long-term goals. Unlike basic training, the Chemical Officer Basic Course (COBC) required long training hours. I needed to be fully alert and able to perform at my best.

The length of time and subject matter was very stressful. I felt very alone. To know I had a fiancé who really didn't care for my chosen profession meant I wasn't about to divulge my fears or burdens to him. I rationalized that he didn't care and wouldn't support me anyway. When I would really need someone to encourage me to persevere to achieve the reward, I felt he'd only tell me to quit. He could sense that I wasn't being very open with him about what was causing my stress.

He said, "Terrina, I feel like you're holding back on me."

I replied, "You're right, I am. I feel like the weight of my military career is entirely upon my shoulders and like I'm doing this by myself. I don't feel like I have your support, because you've told me you don't respect the military. If you don't respect the military, you don't respect me. The military is an extension of me whether you like it or not."

Although he assured me that was not the case, it was evident that the relationship was fizzling out. My emotions had already caught up to the fact that it was ending.

—A Secret Place in My Heart—

Nelson was the first male I had ever allowed into a very secret place in my heart. I had spent a considerable amount of time with him—more than I had ever spent with anyone else. We saw each other every day, almost as if we were married. All my other relationships were long-distance, and Nelson was the only boyfriend I saw daily.

Once I had moved to Clarksville, Tennessee, it was hard even though we had regular phone contact. Because we had shared so much together, when I knew it was time to end the relationship, it was challenging to let him go.

After he graduated from college, Nelson moved back in with his parents until his mother found him a job in Maryland. I resented that because I felt he needed to be more independent. The Bible makes that clear in Genesis 2:24: *Therefore a man shall leave his father and mother and be joined to his wife, and they shall become one flesh.*

If he really was planning to marry me, why would he return to his parents' home? I had to know.

"It's time for you to branch out on your own and do your own thing. You need to stop depending on your parents to be the center focus of your career path, especially if we're trying to build our life together," I told him to no avail.

I noted that things had considerably changed between us. We needed to have a direct and deliberate conversation.

"Is our relationship over or not?" I asked.

His response was shocking. He said he wouldn't have had such a conversation with me, and rather just transitioned into a friendship. "But yes," he said, "it's over." In other words, he would have just gone his separate way, without even telling me it's over.

I couldn't believe it. How could a man transition from engagement to friendship without ever talking to the woman he was to marry?

I had just returned home from work one night and was sitting in my little one-bedroom apartment having this conversation. I felt a deep pain in my heart. I had trusted this man with my heart, my plans, my fears, and my life with a level of access I had not granted to any other. The breakup was more intense than when my relationship ended with Sam. My heartache was both emotional and physical.

After we talked for a few minutes, we both wound up crying. We had not officially ended things, but it was time.

"Well, Nelson, then do me a favor. I know ending this relationship is the right thing to do. I need you to promise me that you will never call me again," I explained. "No matter what urge you get to pick up the phone and call, please don't do it."

I just couldn't see the two of us even remaining as friends. "If I choose to call, then maybe we can be friends," I added. "But until then, I don't feel like I can even enter into a friendship with you right now."

With the help of Pastor Burgess at Little Walnut Grove Baptist Church, I began to pick up the shattered pieces of my heart and move forward. Only a few people knew my story and my situation. Still, I had to try getting out and being sociable. I had things to do and I really wanted to enjoy life, even though my heart was broken, and I was healing from a deep, deep wound.

I guarded my heart during that time like it was secured in Fort Knox. Nelson, on the other hand, got married nine months after we broke up.

Fear seemed to grip my heart to a point where I searched for security in church functions and outings with friends. Casual dating was not the answer for me—but drawing closer to God was. I began journaling in 1997 to release thoughts and emotions held captive for decades. Now I would uncover the lies I believed about myself and God's truth.

Lesson Learned: Relationships Are Difficult Yet Essential.

Nelson and I were young and still trying to discover our identity apart from our parents' influence. I couldn't receive his love for me through the distorted lens I viewed him—a lens of rejection.

The fear of rejection can be crippling if the root cause of it is not addressed. It can wreak havoc in relationships and cause us to live in a state where we never discover our full God-given potential. In Ephesians 2:3, it says we (all mankind) were by nature children of wrath. God is not to blame for the sins of man. It is our sin nature that causes us to sin. The blessing is when we accept Christ as our Lord and Savior. We are then transformed into a new nature.

I have been redeemed by the transforming power of the blood of Jesus, and I have learned to not discard people for the offenses they cause. It may be my display of love that draws them to the Father. That being said, my relationships have healthy limits or boundaries established to avoid repeated abuse.

If God, who desires great intimacy with me, can extend mercy and love, so can I. Ephesian 6:12 says, *For we do not wrestle against flesh and blood, but against principalities, against powers, against the rulers of the darkness of this age, against spiritual host of wickedness in the heavenly places.* There is a spiritual battle taking place, and we cannot fight it in the flesh.

Photo 5: Commissioning Ceremony at Hampton University

CHAPTER 8

My First "Daddy" Figure

Hear, my children, the instruction of a father, and give attention to know understanding; for I give you good doctrine: do not forsake my law. When I was my father's son, tender and the only one in the sight of my mother, he also taught me, and said to me: let your heart retain my words; keep my commands, and live.

—Prov. 4:1–4

After completing the Officer Basic Course (OBC) at Fort McClellan, Alabama, I moved to Fort Campbell, Kentucky. While there, I began attending Little Walnut Grove Missionary Baptist Church just across the border in Clarksville, Tennessee. It was there I met a wonderful pastor, Dr. Leroy Burgess, who I considered to be my first genuine "daddy" figure.

It was the first time I really felt as though I had a church family. I sang in the choir and stayed after services to mingle with people most Sundays and Wednesday evenings. I was a brand-new Christian at that time and full of questions. I would read my Bible and come across a passage that didn't make sense, so I'd write it in my journal. Then I'd visit the church on my lunch hour and ask Pastor Burgess if he would answer the questions for me.

He knew I was really excited about my new faith, and he encouraged me as much as he could. He would answer my questions by pointing to various passages in the Bible to help me understand the context of scripture.

He was so patient and gracious with me. I'm sure I asked him a lot of silly questions, but he never once made me feel bad for asking them. He knew I was searching for truth, and he was more than happy to fan my passion for Christ.

Until then, my reference to a Baptist church had been watching a scene in the movie *Blues Brothers* where John Belushi "sees the light." People were doing flips in the air and somersaults in the aisles. Based on that scene, I just thought anything goes in a Baptist church. No offense to anyone who comes from a Baptist background, but I just never had much exposure to that denomination during my early Christian experience.

I remember when Pastor Burgess was preaching one Sunday, and something he said clicked inside of me. I really wanted to join the church and make a public profession of my faith. So in the middle of his sermon, I just stood up, walked up to the front, and asked him for the microphone. I thought that was what people did when they felt inspired.

Pastor Burgess just said, "Well, this is kinda unusual, but okay."

He passed me the microphone, and I just started talking. I boldly explained how much I had been touched by the church embracing me as a new resident to the area and as a new Christian. I thanked several people for showing me how to walk out my new Christian faith.

With a big smile on my face, I proudly announced that I wanted to become a member of the church family. I passed the microphone back to Pastor Burgess and returned to my seat as everyone started clapping and rejoicing.

Then a few minutes later, Pastor Burgess announced, "The doors of the church are now open for anyone who decides to accept Jesus, desires to join the church, or wants to come up for prayer." But after recognizing my awkward mistake, I just sat planted in my seat. I was so embarrassed when I realized that that was the moment I really should have gone up front.

I must have looked very uncomfortable because an elderly lady kept motioning for me to come up to the front. But I didn't respond to her gestures. I didn't really want to draw any more attention to myself.

After the service ended, the lady sought me out and gave me a big hug. She was all smiles and very friendly. She welcomed me to the church family and assured me that everyone was glad to have me as a member. She made no mention of my blunder.

Pastor Burgess took me under his wing and began to personally disciple me going forward. He knew my heart and even though I didn't know any better or even how to act in church, apparently he understood that too. Like I said, he was so full of grace and patience that it made him an ideal first pastor.

We would frequently meet one-on-one during the lunch hour to talk about the church and the Bible, as well as any life concerns I had. I had just ended a relationship with Nelson, to whom I was technically engaged, but it never felt like an engagement to me. I was embracing the reality that we would not be getting married because Nelson had moved on with his life.

I still had a strong emotional bond with Nelson and was just heartbroken. I was having a hard time understanding that the relationship ended. I remember crying a lot in Pastor Burgess' office. He would patiently listen as I poured out my grief and confusion, just as I imagined a father would listen to his daughter who had just experienced a major breakup.

He helped me process the breakup and tried to help me realize what God wanted for me. A revelation of how I needed to love myself emerged from our conversations. We talked about God's goodness, His love for mankind, and, more importantly, God's love for me.

─Seeing King David as a Role Model─

As a soldier, I was fascinated with the life of King David. He was one of the Bible characters that I really homed in on. It was rather unique. When most people become new Christians, they turn to the Book of John to better understand their new faith and who Jesus is.

But I zeroed in on 1 and 2 Samuel. Because my unit was out in the field a lot, I could completely identify with the challenges David faced leading an army. One of the biggest questions I remember having is how David could be considered a man after God's own heart when he engaged in some of the most hellacious behavior recorded in the Bible.

Pastor Burgess helped put it all into context that good people can do stupid things. That's how I came to understand how our God-given free will allows us to make decisions to go our own way, rather than God's way. Yet even when we do things our way, God keeps pursuing a relationship with us.

I also struggled with the concept of submission and submitting to authority. That's a big issue in the military, and I wondered how my overall perception of men impacted that thinking. I remember asking Pastor Burgess how women were expected to submit to their husbands' authority if the husband didn't seem to like his role or take his responsibility seriously. I wondered how I was supposed to submit to a man I didn't believe deserved my submission if he failed to love me unconditionally.

Using scripture, Pastor Burgess pointed to various examples of godly submission and what it meant. I learned there is a big difference between submission, which means voluntarily yielding to the authority of another, like Jesus did with His Father, and subjugation, which is being brought under control, by force.

He taught me what it means to be a subordinate, and what the

Bible teaches on doing things in obedience to God. For example, Colossians 3:23–24 says, *And whatever you do, do it heartily, as to the Lord and not to men, knowing that from the Lord you will receive the reward of the inheritance; for you serve the Lord Christ.*

So through the life of David, I saw that David was operating under a chain of command, like I was in the military. He willingly submitted to the lordship of God, who gave him the grace and wisdom to serve the less-than-desirable King Saul. David, with all his flaws, sought God for decisions on when to enter battle and how to lead the Israelites. It started to make sense to me.

I was in a period of rapid spiritual growth during the year I attended that church before a career-ending injuring saw me honorably discharged from the Army. I left Fort Campbell and moved to Georgia, but I kept in touch with Pastor Burgess. We'd normally speak on Saturdays when we both had less demands on our schedule.

Pastor Burgess died in 2002. I remember getting the call that he was terminally ill. I left Georgia immediately to see him one last time. He died about 30 minutes before I arrived. I was a mess. When I realized I would never be able to say a final goodbye and tell him again how much he meant to me, tears just poured from my eyes.

He was the first man I ever encountered who had a significant positive impact on my life. He opened my eyes to the amazing Christian faith, patiently guided my first steps, and became a trusted confidant and close friend.

I remember the final conversation we had. I had allowed some former church members to stay with me in Georgia, and he admonished me for not seeking his advice first. Like the advice I would expect from a loving wise father, Pastor Burgess thought it might have a negative influence and cause a disruption in my life.

Lesson Learned: *God Gives Us Friends for a Reason and for a Season or a Lifetime.*

I love my friends for their unconditional love, acceptance, and support. They have truly made a difference in my life.

For many years, God purposely allowed me to have certain friends. Those friends came in the form of people my age as well as people who were older and served as parent figures. Regardless of their age, those wonderful friends poured wisdom into me as a mother or a father might normally do.

It is important to evaluate the role people play in our lives, as they very well may be serving a divine need. For me, it was a need to belong. As a member of the Body of Christ, I am a fellow citizen with those who are of the household of God—His dwelling place exists in me in the Spirit (see Ephesians 2:19–22).

CHAPTER 9

Changing Courses

I am the LORD, that is My name; and My glory I will not give to another, nor My praise to carved images. Behold, the former things have come to pass, and new things I declare; before they spring forth I tell you of them. Sing to the LORD a new song, and His praise from the ends of the earth, you who go down to the sea, and all that is in it you coastlands and you inhabitants of them!

—Isa. 42:8–10

I was fully prepared to make the military a full-time career for twenty years or more; God, however, had other plans.

I repeatedly injured my knees doing calisthenics and drills. I discovered I have chondromalacia, a condition also known as "runner's knee," where the cartilage under the kneecap deteriorates and becomes soft.

After I injured my knee six times in just six years, I knew a military career wasn't going to work, at least as an officer. Continually patching up my knees was not the solution; yet when I contemplated leaving the service, I had to battle guilt and condemnation.

The voices of Nelson and his father resonated within my mind. I wondered if they were right, after all—that the military is no place for a woman and is a waste of a career. I wanted it to be my decision, something I considered from every angle before choosing the best option for my life as well as my career. My health had to be the priority.

Frankly, I was ready to leave the Army even before I arrived at Fort Campbell. I had convinced myself that the military really didn't care much for me as a person. It sounded alluring as a young woman to have a successful career in a male-dominated profession. But I came to realize that it probably wasn't the best career to have if I wanted a family.

In the Army, when you're injured, you're considered to be relatively worthless, and often treated that way. Considering the investment the Army made in me through ROTC and the Reserves, when I was injured and unable to perform as expected, I was treated like a wasted resource. It was evident through the words spoken to me and the tone, as well as the duties I was assigned.

Still, I worked very hard to prove myself. I pressed on, in crutches when necessary, to live up to my responsibilities. But many soldiers and officers consider crutches to be a sign of weakness, and using them brings dishonor to the uniform. There was a commanding officer who gave me the impression that I truly was a "wasted resource."

I found many military members to be die-hard, "hoo-rah" people, and it didn't make sense to me. I believe a person should reflect his or her true personality, but many soldiers I encountered didn't agree.

I wanted to settle down and eventually have children, which would require me to run after them. My ability to do that would decline tremendously if I continued to get injured. So within a year of arriving at Fort Campbell, I made a formal application to process out of the Army. I initiated the medical discharge process in 1993 and was honorably discharged from the Army in April 1994. My Army career would end within six and a half years of entering the Army Reserve, and after serving just over a year as an officer.

After I separated, I wasn't sure what the next step in my career would be. One of my cousins was stationed at Dobbins Air Force Base in Georgia. After she invited me to start over in Atlanta, I packed my belongings into my car. What didn't fit in my car, went into storage.

I shed a lot of tears during that six-hour drive. My heart was still broken after ending the relationship with Nelson, and my dream career had ended too. What, I wondered, had I done to deserve this. Why couldn't I just have a nice life with a loving husband and a rewarding career?

Satan spoke to my insecurities. He tried to get me to agree that I really was a used up, worthless resource for the Army, and a used up, worthless partner for Nelson. The pain cut deep into my soul.

When I arrived in Atlanta, I stayed with my cousin for seven months. Fortunately she had a spare room and appreciated the company. I appreciated the opportunity to live cheaply as I rebuilt my shattered life. I had a hard time finding a full-time job in the biomedical field, so I went to work for multiple temporary agencies looking for short-term assignments, just so I could bring in money.

Although I initially zeroed in on seeking work through an all-encompassing employment agency, I soon discovered agencies that specialized in medical and healthcare placements. It kept the money coming in but assignments were sporadic. Some months I wondered how I would pay my rent, especially when I couldn't find a new placement for several weeks. I even considered getting a roommate.

Eventually I began earning enough that I could afford a place of my own. It was a two-bedroom apartment in an okay neighborhood, but it was mine. My self-confidence rose as I proved to myself that I did have value and that by working hard and delivering results, people really did appreciate the skills I brought to their companies.

However, I remember a low moment in my life that took place one night when I was talking with my old college friend Evelyn who had moved to Albuquerque, New Mexico. My college friends and I were just starting out in our careers, and they appeared to be enjoying some success while I seemed stuck getting out of the gate. Evelyn was like a sister to me, and I confided many of my insecurities to her.

She also knew how I felt about Nelson and remembered how awkward he was. She had some first-hand experience with him too. That night she told me that Nelson had moved to Maryland to start a teaching job and that he was involved in a serious relationship with another woman. In fact, Evelyn had bumped into our mutual friend Justin who said he had been invited to Nelson's wedding.

I didn't know what to make of the news, and I was reluctant to believe her. I assured Evelyn that Nelson was just bragging in hopes that word would eventually get back to me. I proclaimed that I would believe it when it came to pass.

I was surprised Justin never shared the news with me, because all of us had been very close in college. Maybe he was trying to protect my heart.

As the wedding day approached, I remained curious as to whether news of Nelson's engagement was true. I encouraged Evelyn to call Nelson's parents to find out if the rumors were correct. His mother's reaction proved to both of us that Nelson had, indeed, married just nine months after we broke up.

"Well, my son is now married, so I just need for you to understand that he's a married man now," his mother explained to Evelyn, sounding very territorial. "If you are his friend, I'll let him know that you called, but he's married." And she kept emphasizing that he was married repeatedly.

I felt as though I had been slapped hard and that our relationship must have meant nothing to him. For Nelson to go from crying over our breakup to meeting, falling in love, getting engaged and married to another woman in less than a year really did say a lot about his commitment to our relationship.

First, I wondered if I was the only person who was in love during the time Nelson and I were together. I then wondered if the feelings he expressed to me were even real to begin with, or whether he had an ulterior motive in mind. Finally, I began to suspect he had something going on the side all along and I was just too blind to see it.

Once again I felt used, like Nelson was just using me until the right woman for him came along. Confused and hurt, I turned to God for comfort.

"Lord, this really hurts," I cried. "This feeling I have is so foreign that I don't know what to do or how to process this news. Please help me. Help me to sort through these emotions because I don't know what to do."

At that very moment, one of the things God began to reveal to me was that I had put a man into a special place in my heart that only He could occupy. That is why my heart hurt so much I pondered the revelation and said, "Okay, Lord, then You occupy your rightful place in my heart. Do it now! I give it to You. Just tell me where that place is, and take this pain away, because I don't know what to do with it."

It was like a piercing pain—something I never wanted to experience again. From that moment, I began to shield myself and my emotions again. Thoughts of the emotional turmoil that I experienced while growing up consumed me.

God was right, as He always is. I had made a relationship with Nelson the focal point of my life. Nelson had been my source of comfort, advice, and love, not God. I turned to Nelson for affirmation about who I was and for a sense of value as a person. I had put more value on what Nelson thought of me than what God thought of me. My relationship with Nelson became an idol competing with God for attention and priority. Subconsciously I knew I had not placed my trust in God to provide the intimacy I truly was seeking.

I prayed that God would forgive me and restore my relationship with Him. I also prayed that Nelson would be happy in his new life. Immediately God lifted the pain. It was a sensation I had never experienced before.

When God did that, I said, "Lord, I have a couple of other things I want to talk to you about too. You know I have a desire for marriage," I added. "You also know I have a desire for children. You know that I desire all of these things. But now I want to do things your way."

He began to speak to me, and what He told me that night sustained me for many years.

"I do have a husband for you," God said. "You will know him by his heart, for he will have a heart for Me, and I will reveal that to you."

I was highly encouraged. I got up off my knees, wiped my tears away, and just pressed forward. A new mindset was being developed in me toward men. I socialized with them generally in group settings, and built upon this brotherly outlet where I encountered many young men, whether they were in the church or whether they were my long-time friends from high school and college. I saw them not as prospects for a romantic relationship but rather as being like one of my brothers.

Two men in particular, Justin and Derrick, went to my college and also moved to Atlanta after we graduated. They became part of the family unit I was looking for in the Atlanta area.

I decided to get very active in the singles ministry at my church. I'd meet several men with whom I considered exploring relationships. Every time I met someone new, I would go to God and ask if the man could be the one He promised me.

Usually I didn't hear anything and didn't go forward. Some men tried to pursue me, but if their approach was all wrong, I'd shut it down.

It was a relief to trust God to screen my potential suitors.

Lesson Learned: Relationships Can Never Replace God.

When it comes to relationships with men, too many times I made the mistake of placing them in a position that only God should occupy. That was unfair to the men I dated because I put them in impossible situations. After all, I came to understand that Nelson really did love me, but I was too wounded emotionally to accept what he offered as love.

I discovered that when I was searching for certain things from men, I was really searching for God. Only God can reveal an everlasting type of love. He promises to never abandon me. No one can satisfy me the way God does. God is the only one who can provide me with the validation I need.

Also, in Isaiah 42:8–10, we read of former things passing away and new things springing forth, provoking us to sing a new song to the Lord. Since 2012, I have been singing the following prophetic song (inspired words of Mrs. Julia Primus):

Your Gifts and Callings are Given by My Grace

Rest assured that the talents I have given you and the plan I have for your life will never be taken away. I will never remove them from you, nor will I change My mind.

Your gifts and callings are given by My grace, and there is nothing you can say or do to eliminate them from your life.

Any temptation you face has been experienced by other people, so don't think you are unusual. You can trust Me; I will not allow a temptation in your life that you cannot handle. But when you are tempted, I will show you how to escape the power of it, so that you will be victorious.

Your gifts and callings are given by My grace and there is nothing you can say or do to eliminate them from your life.

Photo 6: Standing outside the Buckingham Palace gate during a trip to Europe

CHAPTER 10

Persevering Through the Challenges of Life

The thief does not come except to steal, and to kill, and to destroy. I have come that they may have life, and that they may have it more abundantly.

—John 10:10

Back in 1999 when I was living in Georgia, I was unemployed for more than half a year. Every month was filled with anxiety about where the money would come from to cover my basic living expenses, let alone a mortgage, car payments, and credit cards. Still, somehow money would arrive just in time to get me through.

In the Lord's Prayer, we are told to thank God for our daily bread. That's what it felt like to me—God provided just enough to get me through that one day.

It was during that time when I learned to really depend on Him, to be encouraged by and through Him, and to know that He was my Provider. That period of my life was when I developed great intimacy with God.

Then in 2000, I finally found gainful employment, and my hope was being restored. I would take on a very active presence in my church where I taught a small group study and a Sunday school class every week.

Unfortunately, a heart-wrenching situation occurred and I was asked to step down from a leadership position where I was teaching.

There was a man who became obsessed with me, and he

began to stalk me. I talked to the church leaders and explained that the man seemed infatuated with me.

At one point, I told him, "Look, there's no way that I will ever consider dating you." I was just that direct, but he didn't catch on. He, instead, tried to solicit people to pray that God would open an opportunity for the two of us to be together.

He was making it a point to learn a lot of personal information about me and to really pry his way into my inner circle. I found it to be creepy. So I spoke to another leader at the church, and this person just decided to minimize the situation. Basically, he said I had overreacted and there wasn't any real danger. But the stalker was obsessed with my personal life and he wanted to know as much information about me as he could discover. It made me very nervous.

When the church wouldn't listen, I took out a protective order that required him to remain a safe distance from me. I even had to deliver a copy of the protective order to the church as well as to my job, because he and his family were calling and threatening me. It was a sad situation. I felt that my church family had abandoned me and invalidated my feelings.

I remember having to deliver the protective order to the security department at my job. Afterward, I learned just how obsessed this man had been with learning about me and my family. People would tell me, "You know, Terrina, he once had a conversation with me about your family."

Others would tell me, "When I would share certain things about what was going on in your life, he would be upset that he wasn't aware of some occurrence, as if he was entitled to know the information."

After I had taken the issue out of the church for it to be handled through law enforcement, many people I knew started to share similar stories concerning him. Perhaps they thought the questions were harmless, so I don't fault them for not alerting me to the situation. I suspect that many of them considered it to be just a harmless little crush.

— Church Hurt —

From that point forward, it became a hellacious experience. The Sunday school leader felt like I should have given him more time to address the problem because he was dealing with some personal issues at the time. He felt I jumped too quickly to seek a resolution rather than giving him time to work it through.

This leader also indicated that he didn't believe the man posed a real threat. Because I acted outside of the church, the leader made it a point to tell me I could no longer teach. He accused me of violating the biblical process for addressing concerns as outlined in Matthew 18:15–17:

> Moreover, if your brother sins against you, go and tell him his fault between you and him alone. If he hears you, you have gained your brother. But if he will not hear, take with you one or two more, that 'by the mouth of two or three witnesses every word may be established.' And if he refuses to hear them, tell it to the church. But if he refuses even to hear the church, let him be to you like a heathen and a tax collector.

The church leader told me that I had not taken the issue before the church's leadership in the proper manner. But I had. I first spoke with the stalker directly, then a Sunday school teacher of a class we both attended. Finally, the church leader was the second person I had approached at the church about the situation. The teacher talked to the stalker, but the activity continued. So I approached the second church leader, seeking help.

To accuse me of violating scriptures was worse than the offense by the stalker! He suggested that I didn't give him enough time to approach the stalker. The leader also accused me of involving the secular world in a church matter. Because I involved law enforcement, he claimed that the secular world didn't care about and should not be involved in church matters.

There are laws adopted and allowed by God to protect His people. By seeking a legal solution to the situation, I argued that I hadn't violated any of man's laws or God's laws. By approaching two leaders, I truly attempted to resolve the situation, but I was made to feel like I was the person creating the problem. This was a major stumbling block for me. What if I hadn't done anything and had an unfortunate encounter with the stalker that left me hurt or worse?

The next Sunday, I showed up to teach my class but was removed from the role just as I was about to teach. The leader and his wife pulled me aside and told me I was not to go into the classroom that day.

Although I was hurt and devastated by this demotion, the situation got even worse. I had a teleconference with one of the pastors from the church a few weeks later. He informed me I had to choose a service to attend—either the early morning service or the late morning service. Whichever service I selected, I would not be allowed to attend the other.

I told them that I didn't think that was an appropriate res-olution, because it worked to punish me, the person who had been violated or offended by this brother. They were treating me as though I was the offender.

I found it interesting that the police detective assigned to my case told me, "You know, the problem with church people is that they don't realize when people do things that are against the law. It is against the law. There are laws in place to protect you, whether you are a churchgoer or not. But the church just is not effective when it comes.

to handling things that are of a criminal nature, and this guy's activities are criminal."

That helped me to realize that I was not crazy, and it supported my decision to take out the protective order. While I was teaching, I was also very active in the counseling ministry there, and the leader over that ministry was in alignment with my decision to seek a protective order. He said, "Terrina, it just makes perfect sense. According to what you told me, you didn't violate scripture, you followed it!"

Devastated and humiliated, people started approaching me with unsolicited advice that didn't seem to line up with scripture. I said, "Look, if you are not clearly hearing from the Lord, if God is not telling you to speak to me, with all due respect, please don't share your opinion unless He is leading you to do so."

I was in a very fragile place at that time. I didn't need well-meaning people to inject guilt and condemnation into the situation.

I was protecting my heart against hurtful or confusing words. I was just too vulnerable to possibly make an emotional decision without hearing directly from the Lord. Emotionally drained, I didn't want any other distractions to interfere with that conversation.

Through it all I learned that, yes, the church has a procedure to handle disagreements and personal offenses in the proper way, but there's a fine line between what the church should be able to do and what law enforcement should do.

Unfortunately I became discouraged and uncomfortable worshiping at that church. I felt like I had been shunned by that Christian community. My friendships changed as people started to act a little differently toward me, leading up to my final decision to leave that church.

Lesson Learned: When God Moves in Your Life, Trust That It's the Best Option.

Although, I could have easily decided to run away from the church, I turned to God like never before. In that period, I discovered that while I looked for family members, boyfriends, and the church to define me, God's word revealed my true identity. I just needed to believe what He said of me. I really learned to stand on the promise conveyed in Jeremiah 17:7–8:

> *Blessed is the man who trusts in the Lord, and whose hope is the Lord. For he shall be like a tree planted by the waters, which spreads out its roots by the river, and will not fear when heat comes; but its leaf will be green, and will not be anxious in the year of drought, nor will cease from yielding fruit.*

If you take the time to confirm with God what you think you hear Him telling you, and then you receive that confirmation, you don't need to worry, even when you can't see how it will all work out.

CHAPTER 11

Insight from a Wilderness Experience

But He made His own people go forth like sheep, and guided them in the wilderness like a flock; and He led them on safely, so that they did not fear.

— Ps. 78:52–53

For a long time after that church experience, I didn't feel that anyone really loved me for being me. Worse, I felt like I didn't deserve any love at all. I had agreed with Satan that there was something in my character that made me unappealing to people, and men in particular.

To support this belief, I poured myself into my career where I sought fulfillment in work, sacrificing a social life all together. A job opened in Utah, and despite sensing that it was not the opportunity I should accept, I took the job and moved as far away from my family, friends, and support network as I could. I had no one to lean on, except God.

That's typical of how Satan works. He tries to separate people from the pack—to isolate them and make them wallow in self-pity to the point they are distracted by offenses and unforgiveness.

Even though I made the choice to run away to Utah, God neither wasted the opportunity nor did He allow me to walk too far away from Him. In fact, when it was just God and me, He had my full attention, which is what I assumed He wanted all along.

I remember one day pouring out my soul to God, and He responded, "I want to give you the desires of your heart, but you must be ready to receive them."

That made me smile. I was thinking that God was getting ready to bless me in a way I had desired for a long time. In making me ready to receive those blessings, God had to purge some ugliness and pain from within me.

Over the course of many months of prayer and fasting, God drew out my pain, healed it, and put it all in perspective. For instance, it was there in Utah where I really began to embrace the pain I had experienced from growing up without my father, and for the other relationship challenges I had with Ma and Daddy. It was in Utah that I really came close to God. I didn't have much of a social life there, and I didn't fit in with the Mormon culture that defines that region.

I recall thinking about my stepfather and how I just needed to finally accept the fact that I never had a relationship with him. I needed to release all expectation of what I thought the relationship should be. It was just making us both uncomfortable.

I had to accept the fact that Daddy was comfortable only when relating to me through other people. Likewise, I would only relate to him through other people as well.

Ma would tell me things about what he had done, what his belief system was, and described activities and circumstances that shaped his life. Other members of the family shared a couple of things with me, and that's how I related to him and what I knew about him.

If there was a family gathering, he would be in the midst absorbing firsthand knowledge of me by what I was saying. But we rarely enjoyed a one-on-one conversation.

When it came to Ma, I had to understand that she could

only give to me what she knew how to give. Loving people requires a lot of effort and a willingness to step out of our comfort zone. I believe that has been very difficult for Ma to do, and I accept that.

Randolph and I have a one-on-one relationship. I talk directly to him, not through someone else.

I'm grateful to finally have a relationship with Randolph. Without him, it seemed like a piece of the puzzle of my life had been missing. Now it has finally found its place, and the puzzle is complete.

I've reflected on the word that God gave me in Utah when He spoke to my heart, "I'm ready to give you the desires of your heart, but you must be ready to receive."

Besides unconditional love, which God graciously gave to me without expecting anything in return, the biggest desire of my heart was to have an earthly man to love, support, and guide me. Thank goodness, I can now enjoy such a relationship with my father who was absent for the first season of my life.

Lesson Learned: We Need Intimacy in Our Lives.

I believe God created us for intimacy with Him, and our greatest desires are satisfied in Him only. We all have a need to belong. My search for significance and acceptance has been found in Christ Jesus and the heavenly Father (see Eph. 1:3–6). Learning how to embrace an intimate relationship was first discovered with God. The proper intimacy with the Father certainly prepares me for any earthly intimate relationship.

My natural tendency is to run or withdraw when I am uncomfortable. Oftentimes God has a way of making us uncomfortable such as in *the wilderness* to make us deal with our issues. Similarly, He chose to capture Jonah's attention in the belly of a fish when Jonah tried to *run* from his God-given assignment. It has taken courage to face traumatic events that have happened to me. Healing and deliverance, I believe, will be a daily journey. I have full assurance that God will complete the work He began in me for His glory!

CHAPTER 12

My Family Reunion

Therefore humble yourselves under the mighty hand of God, that He may exalt you in due time, casting all your care upon Him, for He cares for you. Be sober, be vigilant; because your adversary the devil walks about like a roaring lion, seeking whom he may devour. Resist him, steadfast in the faith, knowing that the same sufferings are experienced by your brotherhood in the world. But may the God of all grace, who called us to His eternal glory by Christ Jesus, after you have suffered a while, perfect, establish, strengthen, and settle you.

–1 Pet. 5:6–10

Lord, I thank you for your word today and the insight that flows from it. So much is on my mind, God, regarding what you are doing in my life and my understanding of my purpose and my calling.

That is what I wrote in my journal on June 27, 2011, which was the week before I was planning to meet my father's relatives in person during a family reunion in his hometown. It was an exciting time for me, but it was also an anxious moment, as I didn't know for sure how I would be received.

So in the days before I would meet everyone for the first time, I just opened my heart to God. This is a glimpse into some of those conversations:

"According to 1 Thessalonians 2:12, my purpose and calling is to walk worthy of You as an heir to Your kingdom and Your glory. Father teach me to understand what this means for my life. As I read the second chapter, I focus on the reference made to a nursing mother and a loving father. I know you are stretching me and maturing me. Help me to dwell on this as I go forward. Order my steps and conversations this day and into the July 4th holiday.

"God, I look forward to meeting my family. I pray that I don't get disappointed by any chain of events. Help me to keep You foremost in my thoughts while I am in Louisiana. I pray for my grandmother's strength. I pray for my father's open heart, my stepmother's understanding, my sister's companionship, and the acceptance and welcoming arms of my aunts and uncles.

"Lord, You made this time possible, and I thank You for it. I praise You for giving me favor with my family. I ask that You show me wisdom in the coming days. Reveal what You see fit to me as I prepare for this family reunion."

After I reconnected with my father, I had a strong desire to meet his side of the family. Fortunately my father was agreeable with that, and he gave me the names of family members I could call. Most of his family lives in Louisiana, Texas, California, and a few other states.

Though Ma said she had never met anyone from his side of the family, my aunt told me later that she had held me as an infant.

The first person I remember talking to over the phone was my grandmother, followed by my aunts and uncles, who really embraced me. They enthusiastically invited me to their big family reunion the summer of 2011. I made it a point to attend. They called it a reunion, but it was more of an annual birthday celebration for my grandmother. She was born on July 6, so the event coincided with Independence Day. The event was a giant backyard barbecue that acknowledged her birthday which she enjoyed celebrating with family.

I was living in Utah at the time, and it had been a busy year for me because I was considering going to law school and had traveled to several universities to visit the campuses. In fact, two of my aunts allowed me to stay with them when I visited schools in their areas. They were the first members of my father's family with whom I really connected.

Prior to the reunion itself, I connected with several members of my father's family by phone, email, and on Facebook. I had also prepared photo albums documenting my life from infancy to adulthood, and I sent them to my father and grandmother. It was the best way I knew to connect with them since they both had no computers or smartphones.

By the time I arrived for the event, most of my father's relatives already knew more about me than I did of them. My hope was to make conversation easier with the family members I would eventually meet.

I included some photos of me as a baby as well as pictures of me at birthday parties and other events. School portraits from my time as an elementary student through high school graduation were in the album as well. I included pictures of my college experience and time in the Army. I tried to keep the images in chronological order to show my age progression.

My goal was to use the albums to show how I evolved as a person, and to capture key events in my life. I shipped my grandmother's album to her prior to my arrival at the reunion. She shared it with the rest of the family in Louisiana. As I was assembling the album, I also posted a few of my favorite pictures to my Facebook account. By doing so, family members I connected with on Facebook could identify me before I arrived. As the day for departure approached, I got a little anxious.

I kept hearing Ma's voice in my head proclaiming that I really didn't know these people and they could be dangerous. I wondered if they would reject me as Ma suggested when she planted negative thoughts in my head.

I briefly entertained those thoughts, but I opted to protect myself a bit by arranging to stay with a friend from my days in the military who just happened to live near my father's hometown.

I used her home in Shreveport, Louisiana, as a base, and I rented a car to drive nearly two hours to my grandmother's home in Marion, Louisiana. As I drove, I was full of enthusiasm, but I was also a little nervous as to how I would be received.

I was to meet at my aunt's house, which was just down the street from my grandmother's home. My aunt lived on the corner, so I parked my car and made my way to the front door.

My welcome was everything I had hoped it would be. There was plenty of hugging and happy greetings. My uncles were busy barbecuing something in the back yard. It smelled delicious. As I was introduced to others, they commented about the pictures they saw in the album I prepared for my grandmother. The scene was busy with conversation and laughter between individuals and small groups of my relatives.

It was a bright, sunny day, and the temperature was in the 90s. Most of my family was trying to stay cool. After a while, my aunt offered to drive me to my grandmother's house, which was only about 100 yards down the road.

My grandmother's house was more than one hundred years old but still in pretty good condition. She told me she still drove, which absolutely amazed me. When I arrived at her home, I saw her and my uncle's cars parked under a very old tree.

The first person I encountered at her house was my uncle, who was just as delightful as he could be. A southern gentleman at heart, he asked if I was hungry. He even offered to find a rabbit, kill it, clean it, and cook it for me. For a Wisconsin girl used to eating food purchased in a grocery store, his gesture was a little too much reality for me, so I politely declined and accepted a coca cola beverage instead.

I was escorted into the house where my grandmother was sitting. I discovered that she was shorter than I, and her face was glowing with a big smile. She was just as excited to meet me as I was to meet her.

We hugged tightly, and she asked me to sit down. With a very quiet and soft voice, she began to ask me questions and share stories with me. She mentioned that my father had told her about me many years earlier and had promised that one day we would get an opportunity to meet.

She explained that family was incredibly important to her and that she didn't like to see any divisions within her family unit. By the way she spoke, I could tell she had little tolerance for people who liked to sow seeds of discontent within her family.

"Family is meant to get along and love each other," she advised. Considering my experience, that was great advice.

I could tell that enjoying close, personal family relationships meant a great deal to her. She was very wise and willing to share lessons she'd learned and advice she'd accumulated through many years of life. She was the matriarch of the family, and it was evident.

I brought out a video camera and recorded an impromptu interview with her. I asked her a slew of questions about growing up in a small country town in the south. She described her own parents and her siblings. I learned she was one of the youngest of seven brothers and sisters. Out of the eight of them, she had the most children.

Her mother was the child of a dark-skinned African American woman and a Caucasian man. My great-grandfather was Caucasian. My grandmother was surprisingly dark-skinned. She also told me her own mother's skin was much darker than mine.

It's incredible that the hues in my family range from very dark to very light. My father's family was a beautiful multi-complexion of colors—a truly blended family. A family willing to freely love me.

She described her experience raising eleven children in Marion while her husband worked as a logger cutting down tall pine trees. Because he worked long hours many days every week, she was the family disciplinarian. She shared fond memories of the mischief her children managed to create and the challenges she faced trying to keep them all in line.

It was obvious she needed a lot of energy to chase after all of them, especially the boys, and she still had plenty of energy despite being more than ninety years old. Her children chimed in with stories of their own, which prompted more stories from my grandmother.

It was cute to hear everyone's stories and I am grateful I was able to record them for everyone to remember forever. One of the key reasons I wanted to record the interview was because I felt I had missed out on so much growing up without knowing my father and his entire family. I wanted to honestly portray my grandmother as the woman she really was—a kind, loving, gentle woman who very much loved her family.

I suspected that my grandmother didn't have much time left on earth, and I wanted her to share her stories, memories, and advice while she was still able to do so. By capturing her thoughts, I created a family heirloom that I know will be passed down from generation to generation.

Because everyone thought it was such a good idea to record my grandmother's interview, I wanted to interview everyone else as well. I was glad to do it because I really got to know the members of my extended family.

I asked each person where they fell in the birth order and to describe what they either did for a living or what they enjoyed doing in retirement. They talked about their own children, hobbies, and fond memories of growing up. Some of those memories included heroic actions of certain family members in the segregated south.

By the time the night was coming to an end, I was recording my first cousins, who were all younger than me. They were all happy to share what they enjoyed most in life.

I learned one of my cousins was an introvert who towered more than seven feet tall. He played professional basketball for a while but eventually opted for a career in teaching and coaching. He helped me design my first website and business cards.

Everyone was very engaging and went to extraordinary efforts to make me feel welcome. My mother had been wrong on all counts. Even though I had been out of their lives for more than thirty years, I was accepted and embraced as a member of the family. It felt as though the remaining pieces of my life's puzzle had finally been put in place.

When it was over, my grandmother was in tears. A gathering of her family was the best gift they could have given her. She valued it far more than any trinkets she may have received. I invested two fun, glorious days getting to know my aunts, uncles, and cousins, as well as answering personal questions from them. I had such a good time at the reunion that I attended again in 2012, 2013, and 2015 before I tapered off my attendance. Even so, I formed special bonds with my paternal family.

For example, one of my cousins, Jon, was married and expecting his first child. His wife, Belinda, suffered from lupus. I understand it can be very painful, and Belinda had a very difficult pregnancy, during which she developed some blood clots. I remember her telling me once the pain associated with blood clots is worse than childbirth. I could tell she was very fearful of her condition. But their daughter, Gabriella, was born healthy in 2014.

Belinda was home on maternity leave caring for the baby one

night when Gabriella was just two months old. My cousin was working a night job. As he normally did, he called home on his break around eight o'clock just to check in. But his wife didn't answer, which he thought was strange.

When he arrived home at 4 a.m., he found Belinda on the floor and Gabriella crying, lying in her bassinet with a soiled diaper. The coroner suspected Belinda died early in the evening, and there was indication that she knew something was wrong and was trying to get to Gabriella. She must have been holding a glass of juice when she collapsed because there was a big red stain on the carpet.

I had just started full-time consulting from my home, which meant that I could work anywhere I had electricity and an internet connection. I told Jon that he shouldn't worry about childcare and that I would be happy to care for Gabriella when he returned to work. He wouldn't have to take any time off from his job to tend to his daughter.

He gratefully accepted my offer, and I traveled one hour each way every day to watch Gabriella while he was at work. I did this for several weeks, as we all sort of pitched in as a family to help Jon through the ordeal. I loved being a surrogate mother to Gabriella, and it reaffirmed my strong desire to have a family of my own someday.

Gabriella began bonding with me, and she would get all excited when I walked into the room.

My grandmother's value of family unity was being revealed, and I was able to participate in it!

No family is perfect, but we have a genuine concern and care for one another. After living apart from them for so long, it became important for me to appreciate and love my extended family.

Lesson Learned: God Designed Family to Bring Him Glory.

In reviewing the genealogy of Jesus Christ, it is said that Adam was the son of God (see Luke 3:23–38). Unlike any other creature God created, man was made in the image of God— the Father, Son, and Holy Spirit (see Gen. 1:26). It was God who said that it was not good for man to be alone (see Gen. 2:18). After Woman was made from Man, the Word says a man shall leave his father and mother and be joined to his wife, and they shall become one flesh (see Gen. 2:24). From the beginning, God intended there to be oneness with Him in the family structure where He would relate to mankind.

The Father's original plan was for man to rule over sin. We understand this from His rebuke of Cain for his unacceptable offering:

Why are you angry? And why has your countenance fallen? If you do well, will you not be accepted? And if you do not do well, sin lies at the door. <u>And its desire is for you, but you should rule over it</u> (Gen. 3:5–7).

God's desire has been for man to live a long life (120 years) before Him and have dominion or rulership in the earth. Even though the first family had sinned, God extended unmerited favor (grace), as He was aware of the frailty of mankind. He is just in dealing with our sins, including those that affect families, nations, and world structures. God's glory, or manifested presence, is evident in the family structure when we have found favor with Him.

Regarding my family, I am continuing to respond in forgiveness, love, understanding, and grace. It has been a process of praying for the souls of maternal and paternal family members, and tearing down spiritual strongholds that had been established in previous generations. Now I can accept my role in my earthly family. I am to rule over sin—my own and that within my bloodline.

Photo 7: First corporate job after leaving the Army

CHAPTER 13

Sam Turns on the Charm—Again

He who hates, disguises it with his lips, and lays up deceit within himself; when he speaks kindly, do not believe him, for there are seven abominations in his heart; though his hatred is covered by deceit, his wickedness will be revealed before the assembly.

—Prov. 24:24–26

I really didn't know what real love was supposed to look like, but I believed it had to be something different than what Ma and Daddy modeled for me when I was growing up. Strange as it seems, I fell for a man who treated me similarly to how Daddy treated Ma. Daddy told Ma a lot of lies, and Sam had done the same thing to me.

After I finally broke off the relationship with Sam, it took nearly two years for me to really get him out of my system and to move forward in my life. I graduated from college, earned my Army commission, and started my military career in Kentucky.

One day in 1993, after I had settled into my living quarters, Sam called me to say he really wanted to meet with me again since we both lived in Tennessee. He was so persistent that I finally consented to have dinner with him. I stood him up and felt good about doing so. He called me later to ask what had happened and to tell me how hurt he was by the snub. I simply told him that something came up at the last minute. I just left it at that, and he soon faded away again.

Fast forward twenty-two years. It was 2015, and I was living in

Dallas when Ma called to tell me that a man named Sam had called her house looking for me. He gave her his phone number and asked that she contact me and relay the message.

I learned later that he had continued to call Ma's house for years after we had broken up, but she stopped giving me the messages. Against my better judgment and more out of curiosity than anything else, I returned his call.

He was so excited that I called. He said he'd been thinking about me all those years. Slowly he reentered my life, and we found ourselves on a fast track relationship—again. He had such a clever way of lying. But because I remembered how deeply in love I was with Sam when I was nineteen years old, I gave him another chance, thinking he might have changed.

Back in 1993, he knew I had accepted Jesus Christ as my Lord and Savior. Now twenty-two years later, he told me that he became a Christian too. He had been married and had several children who were all adults, except for a nine-year-old girl who was a surprise. Sam was now divorced. He placed all the blame for the problems with his marriage squarely on his ex-wife. He described his time with her as "hellish."

I confronted him. "You know, Sam, I have been listening to you for almost twenty minutes, and you've offered no insight into your role in the breakup of your marriage. You've described it as being completely her fault. It is very suspicious to me that you did nothing at all that could have contributed to the failure of your marriage."

He held his ground in blaming his ex-wife. It was like pulling teeth to get him to admit that he could have spent more time with her. "Well," he said, "if you let her tell it, she would probably say I didn't spend enough time with her or do enough to take care of the kids."

He never really owned up to a role in the divorce or never even acknowledged that she probably had a point. The mature, wise response would have been that if she felt that way, it was probably true, and she needed more time from him for the marriage to be successful. But he was incapable of admitting his role, and that told me he had never really healed from the divorce.

Then he started to twist the truth to manipulate my perception of his conduct in his failed marriage. He admitted that she was so distrusting of him that she started checking his phone to see if there were any numbers of other women stored in his list of contacts. He said she was always accusing him of cheating on her and always checking up on him to make sure he was where he told her he would be. She would check his clothing and go through his emails. But he swore he wasn't unfaithful to her in any way.

"When she decided to divorce me, it was right around the time I was planning a trip to Texas with my buddies," he explained, noting it was an annual trip.

I found it to be an incredulous story. "You mean that rather than planning vacations with your wife and kids, you were planning vacations with your buddies, so you could leave your family to have fun with your friends?" I asked. He had a very selfish mindset.

Then he started to complain about how his wife never saved any money, but Sam saw no irony in spending money on a road trip with his friends. He explained that when he returned from the trip, he discovered that his wife and kids were gone. He said he begged and pleaded with her to reconsider, but she was adamant about leaving. He said they had tried counseling, but it didn't work.

"Well, Sam," I said, knowing there was something wrong with the story, "a woman just doesn't wake up one day and decide she needs to be paranoid that her husband is cheating on her. She just doesn't begin to check his phone and go through his clothing on a whim. She must have had a reason to suspect something."

I finally asked him outright if he had been unfaithful to his wife. His answer was weak.

"Well, if she had taken care of her business, no I wouldn't have cheated on her. But she stopped sleeping with me at some point in our marriage, so, yeah, I slept with a lady from work. But it was only after my wife refused me," he explained, thinking that would make it an acceptable excuse. Then he turned on his legendary charm.

"Terrina, I learned so much through that ordeal. I really desire to be married, and I want my marriage to work. The next go around will be much different. I know that." he said. When I pressed him on the lessons he had learned, he said that there needed to be more communication and more love in a relationship. He was speaking to the desires of my heart, and I was falling for him again. He then started listing all the things he loved about me.

I wasn't head over heels in love with Sam, but I wondered if his reappearance in my life was a sign from God that he was the man I was supposed to marry all along. Besides, he continued to talk about marrying me in almost every conversation. It wasn't long before we began addressing the distance between us—I lived in Dallas, and he lived in Antioch, Tennessee.

He couldn't move because of his relationship with his nine-year-old daughter. He wanted to be there and available for her. Again, he was speaking to a desire of my heart—a solid, close father-daughter relationship.

I convinced myself that as the girl's stepmother, I would want her father to be very involved in her life and remain a true father figure, not a guy who called his daughter a few times every month. I didn't have children, and I could easily work from home. Moving to Tennessee would not be a challenge.

Sam spoke to my father and told him that he intended to marry me. He flew out to Dallas to spend time with me and to meet my father's side of the family at a barbecue over Father's Day weekend. But there was an episode that weekend that should have raised red flags.

When I learned he was flying out to see me, I planned a special day. He was planning to arrive early that morning, so I prepared breakfast and scheduled a host of other activities. We were going to do some golfing, walk along a trail, and visit some local museums. It was going to be a day for just the two of us.

When he arrived around eight o'clock that morning, I started cooking breakfast and turned on the TV for him to watch. He turned to me and said, "Terrina, I'm looking at you, and we've been talking all this time, and you haven't even hugged me or kissed me or anything. Can I have a kiss?"

He was right. I had simply greeted him as a friend. So I agreed and nervously walked to the living area where he was standing near the sofa. We kissed for a few moments, but then he forced himself on me. I said, "No, let go. No, we cannot do this. No. We need to go!" But he just pinned me down and had his way with me.

Prior to that encounter, we had talked several times about how I was celibate, saving myself for my future husband. He seemed to be incredibly intrigued by that. He was curious about what it might be like to have a physical relationship with an adult woman who hadn't experienced intimacy in a significant period of time.

After he assaulted me, he said, "You know, no one can be celibate. Look at you."

I thought, *Whoa, I can't believe he just said that to me.*

He implied that the Word of God is not completely correct and that no one can really refrain from having sex, which was a strange thing for a professing Christian to say. Sam told me that we're all sexual beings who just need to give in to those urges.
I was shocked by what had taken place. I didn't call it what it really was—rape—but I immediately started thinking that I had to make it right. After all, if I was saving myself for my husband and we had been talking about marriage plans, then we really needed to move along that path considering what h a d happened.

I asked him, "What does this mean now concerning us?" "Terrina, I still intend to marry you," Sam assured me. "Just slow down and realize that we need to take things slow."

I reminded him that it was too late to just take it slow. I pressed him to define our relationship by asking if we were in a courtship or if he considered us to be engaged.

He assured me that he was fully intending to marry me, but he said I needed to be patient. Yet I felt like his whole disposition changed.

In my mind, I saw our relationship as something that needed to be fixed or corrected because of the sin we had just committed. Sam didn't seem to share my anxiety.

Before he arrived in Dallas, we were communicating five times a day, lasting ten to fifteen minutes each. After he returned to Antioch, the days stretched between each call.

When I questioned the change, Sam reminded me that he never admitted to being talkative on the phone. That was a lie. Again, I was told I needed to relax and not to worry. He assured me again that we would be married someday. I just couldn't be in a rush.

In my effort to fix the situation, I started to look for career opportunities in Tennessee. An opportunity soon presented itself in the Memphis area. I called Sam to tell him about it. I explained that it wasn't the greatest career move for me, but it could be a stepping stone, and it would allow us to be closer together.

"You need to let me know if I'm being too hasty to even consider you in this decision. There are too many things at stake," I told him.

"No, no, no, Terrina," he said. "You know I want to marry you, and I think this will be good for us. It'll be certainly easier with you being in Memphis instead of Dallas. Three hours is definitely better than seven hours, so, yeah, this'll be good for us."

With this response from him, I moved forward in the job interview process. The ball started rolling quickly. I had a phone interview a few days later, then a face-to-face interview the following week. I must have impressed them because the company extended an offer to me and wanted me to start work within thirty days.

I packed up my apartment in Dallas, moved to Memphis, and started a new job within a month. I did so only after Sam assured me that marriage was the direction he wanted to go. Like Eve in the Garden of Eden, I had been deceived by a snake.

Lesson Learned: When People Wrong You, Forgive Them, Even if it is Hard to Do So.

Sam hurt me more than any other person on this planet. Not only had he raped me in Dallas but also had he two more times in Tennessee. I had uprooted my life to be closer to him, and he rejected me within months of moving to Tennessee. He had mistreated me once, and I broke up with him. Many years later, I gave him another chance only to be physically and emotionally abused.

There was an important lesson about forgiveness here. My second experience with Sam was a low point in my life. I forgave Sam yet had a terrible time forgiving myself. I kept rehearsing the following thoughts:

> *Why didn't you trust your instinct that something had been wrong with his failed marriage? How could you allow this man to lie to you again? Your vow of celibacy is broken and you can't be an example of a true Godly woman. You've lost your credibility. You should have known to call what he did to you rape and taken the appropriate action.*

I learned there was a generational pattern of perversion and incest established in my family. Manipulating behavior was a common trait I saw in my parents, and it caused me a great deal of confusion. I often acknowledged bad behavior as normal. Many of my responses to men had been modeled after what I witnessed as a child.

I had been manipulated and emotionally abused by the most important woman in my life—my mother. I had also been manipulated and physically and emotionally abused by one of the most important men in my life—Sam. All I wanted was to be loved and accepted by them.

Looking back, my choices of men in my life were an attempt to get some of the love, attention, support, and affection that I wanted from my father. Key men in my life, like my stepfather, father, and Sam, all had a problem with alcohol.

There lies the pattern of abuse.

Still, I would respond much in the same way my mother did, by minimizing the impact of the abusive behavior. After I returned to Dallas, I knew I had to forgive Sam and the other people in my life who had hurt me, or I would wind up being paralyzed by bitterness and anger.

I remember intentionally telling God that I forgave each of the people who had hurt me deeply. When I would dwell on their roles in my life, God would remind me to forgive them again. I then realized something else was at work in me—soul ties that had to be broken.

A soul tie is a bond that is formed between two people, like a husband and wife, a child and parent, or two friends. The souls of the two people become united. These bonds can either be healthy or unhealthy. Healthy soul ties in scripture are revealed in Matthew 19:5: *For this reason a man shall leave his father and mother and be joined to his wife, and the two shall become one flesh.*

It can also be seen in 1 Samuel 18:1: *Now when he had finished speaking to Saul, the soul of Jonathan was knit to the soul of David, and Jonathan loved him as his own soul.*

Whereas an example of an unhealthy soul tie can be found in Genesis 34:2–3, the rape of Dinah: *And when Shechem the son of Hamor the Hivite, prince of the country, saw her, he took her and lay with her, and violated her. His soul was strongly attracted to Dinah the daughter of Jacob, and he loved the young woman and spoke kindly to the young woman.*

In my case, the soul ties with my mother and with Sam were very unhealthy.

Along with forgiving others, I worked to forgive myself by seeking out inner healing and deliverance through organizations such as Denton County Friends of the Family and Mining the Truth Deliverance Ministries. Inner healing and deliverance over deep-rooted traumatic experiences has been a daily process. I'm honest with myself about how I feel while allowing God to heal the inner wounds layer by layer.

Photo 8: Sailing on Lake Lanier in Georgia

CHAPTER 14

Following My Heart, Not God's Plan

A man's heart plans his way, but the Lord directs his steps.

—*Prov. 16:9*

"Terrina, you move way too fast," Sam told me a few days before I planned to move to Memphis.

I had accepted the job and the company was planning on me being at my desk in less than a week. I had given notice to my apartment, and my household goods were on their way to Memphis. There was no turning back.

"That's the way my career works, Sam," I explained. "When a company finds my skillset meets their need, a decision is usually made quickly."

"It's just moving faster than I expected, that's all," he assured me after I asked if it was still the direction he wanted to go. "I love you, Terrina. I intend to marry you."

Sam was concerned about the speed at which we were reuniting. He was just as surprised as I was that the move was coming together so quickly.

I had already vacated my apartment, and I was wrapping up loose ends in Dallas when Sam called me one day. "You know, Terrina, I would hate for you to take that job and move on account of me."

I was ready to explode. "I know darn well you're not having this conversation with me after I packed up all my belongings and they are on their way to Memphis," I snapped. "How dare you make a comment like that! You are the primary reason I'm moving to Tennessee in order to start a new job. What are you trying to say?"

Sam began a song and dance reassuring me that he loved me yet saying over and over that I was moving too fast. Fast? Did he not speak to my father and explain his intentions to marry me in hopes of receiving my father's blessing? He assured me again that he meant every word and was really, truly in love with me.

I was unsettled in my heart the entire drive to Tennessee. When I arrived, I sensed Sam was very uncomfortable with my presence. It was as though he thought he could just flip a switch on when he wanted me to be a part of his life, and then flip it off when he changed his mind.

For a month, I stayed in a corporate housing complex in an upscale neighborhood. I needed to sign the lease, complete a walk-through, and get the keys. Sam was agitated about everything, it seemed. He kept complaining about how long it was taking, and he finally stormed off to wait outside.

There was absolutely no reason for his behavior. It was as though his entire personality shifted from a warm, loving, excited Sam one day to an agitated, worrisome Sam the next.

I was in denial as to what was transpiring. I wasn't seeing the relationship in its true perspective or how he was abusing me.

While I was in Tennessee, he assaulted me two more times. One time he asked, "Don't you want this?" When I told him I did not, he seemed incredulous. "You don't?"

When I told him again that I did not, he replied, "Oh, well, I can't stop. Let me finish." He did his business, but he had a guilty look on his face when he was done. He never apologized or admitted that what he had done was wrong. His actions demonstrated a complete disrespect for me and disregard for my desires.

There really was no love present in our relationship, just fear and deception.

When he saw me face-to-face, he often displayed an attitude of resentment. I believe he was beginning to see that we weren't compatible after all, and stayed aloof.

Deep, deep in my heart, I wanted to be married. I had been single for a long time. God had promised me a husband. Sam was my chance not only to be married but also to help raise a little girl. Perhaps my motive was to help bring God's promises to pass, like Sarah having Hagar to conceive a child for her (see Genesis 16:1–4).

—Fighting the Tide—

It was extraordinarily odd that Sam didn't want me to meet his kids. In order to see him, I was always the one to travel. It was a three-hour trip to Antioch, and three hours back. Sure, he'd have something ready for me to eat when I arrived, but his personality was rather cold and distant.

His youngest son was nineteen years old at the time. He dropped by unexpectedly while I was there one day. He let himself into Sam's home and startled me in the kitchen. We conversed before he retreated to his bedroom. He was a very nice young man. To my surprise, Sam was offended that I had spoken with his son.

Sam told me that it was his plan to sit down with his kids as a group to tell them about me and then to formally introduce me to them. I wondered why that conversation couldn't have taken place during the thirty days I was transitioning from Dallas to Memphis. "Sam, that doesn't make any sense to me. We're in the same space. What would you prefer I do, ignore your son when he comes into your home and I'm here with him? Why wouldn't you want me to speak to him? More importantly, why wouldn't you want him to know who I was?" I questioned. Though deep inside, I knew the answers.

Despite promising that his next marriage would be different in that he'd spend more time with his wife and family, and be more loving, I discovered that he put everything else before our relationship. His children, his job, finances, golfing, and every other type of pleasure would come before me.

"I fall lower on the totem pole in your life than golf," I told him one day. "I'm just someone who is available to you when it's convenient for you. How dare you!"

I felt so betrayed and tossed aside. I wondered if there was some characteristic in me that attracted manipulative, abusive men. It took so much of my energy to stay composed at work or wherever I went because I just wanted to cry. Crying myself to sleep became a nightly occurrence in Tennessee.

I don't believe Sam was a Christian. At least he didn't seem to be living a lifestyle of someone who was a committed Christ follower. We had one Bible study together, and that was by phone when I was still in Dallas. He never talked about Christian things, biblical insights, or issues from a Christian perspective. We only went to church together once.

His actions and speech were not adding up.

"Terrina, I never meant to hurt you, and I am sorry," he told me one day. "I should have spoken up about you taking the job on account of me."

This confession came months after I already resided in Tennessee. Inwardly, I resolved that the relationship was over. There was no need for me to invest anymore time trying to fix something doomed from the beginning.

"I uprooted my life based on your lies," I said to him one night. He replied, "You didn't have to do that. It was a choice you made by yourself." I was angry that he would deny he agreed the move would be good for our relationship.

To add insult to injury, I felt that he measured his acceptance of me as a wife by his ex-wife's past or present actions. He mentioned that his ex-wife would always be in his life, even though she moved on and remarried. He even admitted to paying for a life insurance policy for her. A friend tried explaining that he probably did that so that if something happened to her, and he needed to raise their daughter, he'd have some income to help.

Also, Sam said he paid for life insurance policies for each of his adult children. Something wasn't adding up. Then it dawned on me like the light from a sunrise.

He didn't love me. He wanted a nurse—a sugar mama—someone to pay all his bills and take care of him as his health declined. That was why I was so attractive to him. As a professional with a good income, I could provide him with the lifestyle he dreamed of having.

In my quiet time, I confessed my blindness to the Lord. All the writing was on the wall. Dozens of red flags had been raised, and I was too blind to see them. Or, even if I saw them for what they were, I was willing to either ignore their presence or rationalize their significance.

I lasted just seven and a half months in Tennessee before moving back to Texas.

The relationship with Sam was no longer in question. He wouldn't be an asset to my life in any way. I needed to leave, but I had already made a commitment to the job. That's when God stepped in again.

As quickly as circumstances unfolded to usher me to Memphis, they unfolded to open the door for my return to Dallas.

With Sam out of the picture and no longer a factor in my life, the new job I accepted was still a magnet holding me to the area.

My short time at the company was a vivid reminder as to why

God pulled me out of the dog-eat-dog corporate environment, and He directed me into business for myself. I no longer felt like navigating bureaucracies anymore.

Once I grew accustomed to setting my own schedule and working with whomever I wanted, the transition back into the corporate workforce was not an easy one.

I was at a stage in my life where I wasn't willing to invest a lot of time and energy to see if a situation could be changed in a year or two. It was so much easier, and far more enjoyable, to run with a synergistic and passionate team focused on completing a project or goal than it was to drag them reluctantly along a path.

It took a few trips to Dallas to secure a new apartment. Within two weeks, I secured a lease remotely, reserved a U-Haul truck, and towed my car and all of my belongings back to Texas. I paid movers in Memphis to load the truck and car for me; then paid movers in Texas to unload it all.

Once I realized that God was allowing my exit, there was no need for hesitancy. It was time to act. I was done with Sam. There was no redeeming value to even maintain a friendship with him.

Sam called me on my birthday. He had no idea I had moved back to Texas, and he was literally stunned upon hearing the news. He started in with a bunch of sob stories as to what was going on in his life.

He didn't get very far before I interrupted him. "Sam, if you started with lies, continued with lies, and ended with lies, it is obvious nothing you say can be trusted," I explained. "Haven't you wondered why I never bothered to pick up the phone to see how you were doing? I'm not calling you at all, for any reason. There is nothing of value in these conversations for me. You had the opportunity to tell me how you truly felt before I left Dallas and moved to Memphis. Instead, you lied to me and led me to believe you loved me and wanted to marry me."

A wise girlfriend of mine was quick to counsel me against allowing unforgiveness, anger, and bitterness to take root in my heart. If Sam called me today, I'd be unshakable. There would be no negative emotions at all.

Because he tended to reach out to me every few months or so, I saw future attempts by Sam to contact me as a way for Satan to lure me into another emotional response, whether good or bad. Just a simple conversation with Sam was often enough to elicit a response within me. I had fully released him, but he kept trying to ease his way back into my life.

When I bought a new phone, I forgot to block his number. One day I answered a call without recognizing his number. He was carrying on conversations with others around him while on the phone with me. I told him I had to turn my attention to another matter, and I promptly ended the call.

He sent me a text a few days later to tell me a special older woman in his life had died. When I saw that text, I knew he was attempting to see if the doors of communication could remain open with me, which was something I didn't want.

"Lord, I don't want to fire off a nasty, mean-spirited response to Sam, but I don't want him to contact me ever again. What can I do?" I prayed.

I was led to reply, "My condolences to you and your family members as you grieve. I pray that God will comfort you. Please keep in mind, I don't mean this in a negative way, but don't ever contact me again."

That was it. He has not contacted me since.

Lesson Learned: If You Ask God to Remove the Pain, He Will.

Going before the Lord whenever my heart had been shattered into pieces by the hurt others caused me has been some of my most comforting experiences. God has never disappointed me when it comes to wrapping His loving arms around me.

Rather than repeat what was mentioned on soul ties in the last chapter, I will say there were demonic forces at work that tried to hold me captive. Unknowingly I had agreed with the lie that I wasn't worthy of love and that I had to earn the love of a man.

God reveals Himself to us through His Word (or Logos). Allowing God to reveal His truth about who I am, as opposed to emphasizing accusations of the enemy, has been key to my inner healing. Every day the enemy will accuse us. Nevertheless, Revelation 12:10 states that salvation, strength, the kingdom of our God, and the power of His Christ have come. I have assurance that I am not abandoned or cast down. Instead, I am an overcomer through the redemptive blood of Jesus Christ.

The guilt and shame I felt from the repeated abuse I endured was finally replaced with revelation that God loves me with a pure, unconditional love. That which I was seeking, I could find in Him.

CHAPTER 15

Breaking Curses: the Road to Healing

And I will give you the keys of the kingdom of heaven, and whatever you bind on earth will be bound in heaven, and whatever you loose on earth will be loosed in heaven.

— *Matt. 16:19*

As I matured as a Christian, I came to understand and really appreciate the power of the spoken Word of God, as well as the need to set healthy boundaries in my life. It is essential that we break curses spoken against us and agreements we have accepted as being true statements about us; otherwise we give Satan authority to hold us in bondage or to harass us our entire lives.

If we want deliverance from the issues in our past that have held us back and prevented us from becoming all we really could be, we must deliberately accept God's truth and reject the accusations of Satan or any demonic force. What's done is done. We can't change our past; we can only accept it and move on.

2 Corinthians 5:17 is a powerful passage that encourages us: *Therefore, if anyone is in Christ, he is a new creation; old things have passed away; behold, all things have become new.* We must embrace the new!

If we continue to act like our old, hurt selves, we stifle our new growth. What happened in my youth was totally out of my control. I may have contributed to what happened to me as an adult, but I have a choice to either dwell upon my mistakes and play the role of a victim or accept God's empowerment to move on and live a new life.

─Cursed in the Womb ─

Parents don't realize that they can actively curse their children with their thoughts, attitudes, and words even before they are born. A child can likely sense when he or she is wanted, loved, and desired, as opposed to being unwanted, despised, and rejected as an unplanned hassle.

I suspect that my mother did that since I was an unplanned pregnancy. Whether it was intentional or not, I have learned that she spoke words over me while I was in her womb. Speaking aloud negative words or phrases, like "I wish I had never become pregnant" or "I really didn't want to have this child," opened the door to demonic influences in my life.

1 Peter 5:8 reminds us to be sober and vigilant, as our adversary the devil walks about like a roaring lion, seeking whom he may devour. What better way for Satan to destroy a person's potential than by ambushing him or her before emerging from the womb!

Negative words work as a spoken curse over a person's life. The baby emerges from the womb into an environment where he or she is considered a nuisance. Being rejected at birth, the child immediately senses it is unloved and unwanted. Even babies sucking at their mother's breast or from a bottle can tell the difference between a loving embrace, soothing caresses, or affirming words and simple, necessary nourishment delivered in anguish. The infant brings those subconscious thoughts into childhood. As the child begins to understand language, he or she picks up on words of anger and associates them with the parent's attitude toward the child. The infant or toddler feels rejection. The baby senses he or she is unwanted and unworthy of a parent's attention or affection.

Proverbs 18:14 asks, *The spirit of a man will sustain him in sickness, but who can bear a broken spirit?* If a child is not accepted, he or she immediately senses rejection and a feeling of not belonging to a family group. Left unresolved, those feelings cement into an ironclad agreement.

—The Orphan Spirit—

The result of that rejection is the creation of a broken spirit, sometimes called an orphan spirit. It all takes place at the subconscious level, even before the child begins to communicate. It is like having a wounded spirit, which takes the joy out of living. A broken spirit removes hope and purpose from life.

A child with a broken spirit will spend much of his or her life trying to bring order to the chaos. He or she may operate in rebellion and become very strong-willed and disobedient. Naturally suspect of others, it will be hard for that child to submit to authority—and almost impossible to accept love, even from God. That child may experience a lot of loneliness.

The child will sense that affection and love is the direct result of behavior, not something he or she receives unconditionally. The child must become a people pleaser in order to avoid offending or angering another person. It is the only way the child learns to be accepted. A child with an orphan spirit sees love as something he or she attains, not as something freely given.

Many people with an orphan spirit become overachievers. They get affirmation only from their own effort. In order to be accepted they must become well-accomplished and set high standards for themselves.

One of Satan's most effective strategies is to convince someone he or she is not worthy of love or acceptance. The enemy's lies, such as "you are a mistake, you are an accident, you have no potential, no one wants you, or you are not worthy," are especially effective when deployed during childhood.

If a child hears those lies enough, he or she will begin to believe it. And if a child hears words like that from a parent, those words become the foundation upon which his or her entire life is built. The child realizes he or she is odd, weird, out-of-place, or different. The child learns it is essential to improve the lives of others in order to be accepted by them, as failure to do so is continued rejection.

The cycle of failure feeds off itself. It cements the child's negative self-image and self-esteem. The child becomes angry, sullen, and withdrawn simply because he or she doesn't live up to self-imposed standards. In reality, the child rejects him or herself. Subconsciously the child agrees he or she is unworthy even of self-love.

When growing up in that environment, a teenager can either withdraw inward to self-imposed isolation or become the "life of the party," thinking performance is the only way to gain acceptance.

—The Most Effective Weapon—

This is not just a small spiritual battle being waged around a child with a broken spirit; it is an all-out spiritual war! For we do not wrestle against flesh and blood, but against principalities, against powers, against the rulers of the darkness of this age, against spiritual hosts of wickedness in the heavenly places (Eph. 6:12).

A child with a broken spirit doesn't stand a chance of over-coming the internalized attitudes and mental agreements made regarding unworthiness, UNLESS that spirit is replaced with another spirit—a Holy Spirit—that can work like an eraser to nullify those agreements with a new paradigm.

Even if another human being, like a parent, is used to foster or create that sense of unworthiness, the battle is being played out behind the scenes in an epic collision between good and evil.

The most effective weapon I have discovered against that type of spiritual oppression requires the Holy Spirit. It is impossible to escape without deploying the weapon of forgiveness. It is forgiveness that breaks the chains that keep people bound to their past and attached to unholy self-accepted beliefs.

Forgiveness was at the core of my own inner healing and deliverance. I had to forgive my mother, stepfather, father, boy-friends, and others—sometimes many times before the chains were truly broken.

I had to forgive Ma for her very negative style of communication, which repeatedly wounded me. I discovered that fear was likely at the core—fear that she had to work to achieve love for herself, even from me, and fear of being hurt.

I had to forgive Daddy for being so distant with me and for being unwilling to demonstrate love in a healthy way. I suspect he wasn't taught about forgiveness either. He, too, had traumatic experiences in his life and was challenged with self-esteem and self-image issues. His relationship with me has been like a social media presence that doesn't really allow two people to get to know each other well; although it is possible for someone to watch another's life without getting personally involved.

I also had to forgive Randolph for abandoning me in infancy, even though it wasn't entirely his fault. He, too, was wounded and rejected by others, including my mother. He may not have been taught the secret of forgiveness. Actually, he still struggles to accept the forgiveness I gave him. His pain runs deep, and the only way he knows to soothe that gnawing discomfort is through alcohol.

Both Randolph and Daddy had a responsibility to provide a covering for me as a child. It was their duty, and they dropped the ball. I can either dwell upon their failures or forgive them and move out of the darkness of my past and into the glorious future my heavenly Father has in store for me.

The human failures of my earthly father and stepfather shaped and formed my relationships with men, whether they were family, friends, classmates, boyfriends, or employers. Any earthly father can even influence the type of mate a child selects as an adult by modeling the right partner.

How a father responds to life works to shape how a child responds to life. It especially shapes how that child even receives love. If a father's love is tainted, because that's all he ever experienced, then that's what the child will gravitate toward. A father's influence can work as a magnet to attract healthy or unhealthy things to his children—especially in youth, but also through adulthood.

It is a lot of responsibility, and, frankly, most men are incapable of living up to the challenge, because they, too, have been hurt. But there is hope.

Forgiveness Is an Ongoing Process

The most important thing about forgiveness is that it is not a one-and-done type of activity. For me, it is an ongoing process. It requires going before the Lord and asking Him to reveal the lies I have believed about myself, about others, and, most importantly, about God. Only God can work to exchange those lies for His truth.

Because it is a spiritual war, it requires active engagement to defeat the enemy. The good news is that God fights the battle for us. We just need to get close to Him and allow Him to shield us from the attacks of our common enemy. 1 John 4:4 promises that *He who is in you is greater than he who is in the world.*

As we get closer to God, He gives us power to refute and renounce Satan's lies and to cast them before the feet of Jesus.

Every time Satan tries to conjure up thoughts about past hurts and people who have let us down, we must take those thoughts captive and subject them to God's Word. When we make our thoughts obedient to God's Word, then Satan's lies melt away. They can't stand up against God's refining fire.

Slowly, by addressing one lie or unholy agreement at a time, God has restored my fragmented heart. He has done a beautiful job in reconstructing my heart to line up with how He truly feels about me. Throughout my journey of healing, He has shown me the truth to overcome each of Satan's lies.

There are still areas of my life that may need His healing power. But I can trust God to bring them to my attention at just the right time, so I can confess my role in agreeing with the lies, forgive someone for hurting me, and accept God's grace, mercy, and healing. I know God will show me time and time again that He is the father I have longed to have in my life.

It is through this ongoing rapport with my heavenly Father that God imparts wisdom to me, as well knowledge. In Matthew 5:48, Jesus promises us that we will be perfect, just as our Father in heaven is perfect. It is a process that takes a lifetime by progressing one step at a time.

With God as the perfect father, He will protect you, shield you, guide you, and allow you to feel connected.

With your heavenly Father by your side, you no longer have to feel lonely, because He is with you—always. You no longer have to feel abandoned, because He will never leave you. You don't have to feel rejected, because God has accepted you, and that is all that really matters. You plus God is more than enough. You are not a mistake. While your family may have rejected you, God has adopted you. Your birth may not have been planned, but God created you in your mother's womb intentionally and for a specific purpose—for a mission to be accomplished, in this lifetime, at this specific time and place.

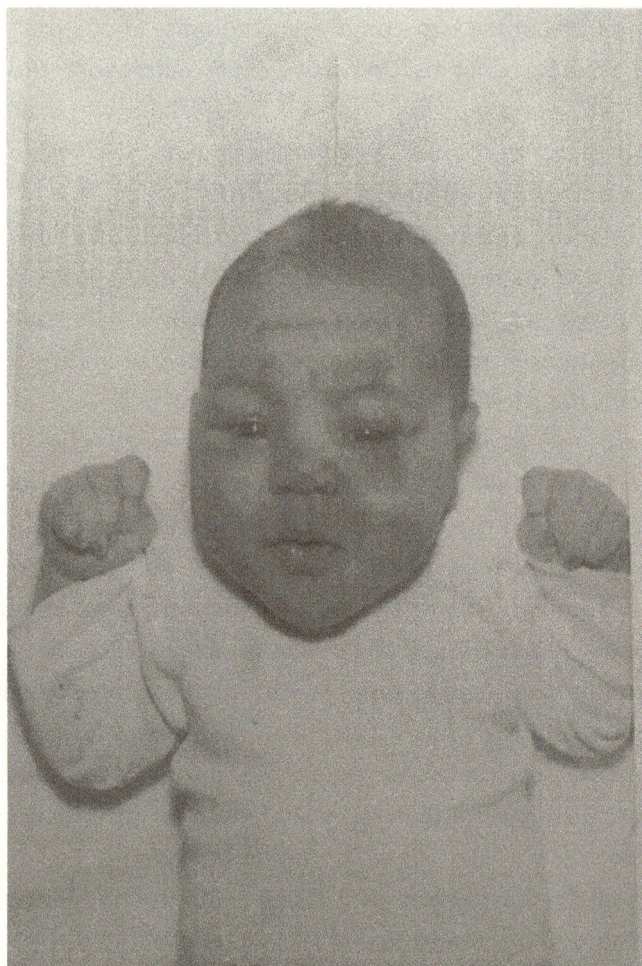

Photo 9: Me as an infant (2 months)

CHAPTER 16

Journaling: An Intimate Connection with the Father

Now this is the confidence that we have in Him, that if we ask anything according to His will, He hears us. And if we know that he hears us, whatever we ask, we know that we have the petitions that we have asked of Him.

—1 John 5:14–15

I don't remember what prompted me to start journaling in 1997 about revelations I gained from my Bible study and prayer time with God. It has proven to be one of the most intimate activities I do on a regular basis.

When I simply need to be recharged, I can just pick up the Bible and begin combing through the Word for a few moments of personal devotion.

I attend church because I enjoy my time with fellow believers, and I usually get something out of the messages delivered during the services. But the key ingredient for developing the close, personal relationship I have with God is found in the private, intimate devotions that I have with Him. Journaling really helped me in that regard.

When I would read a passage, and something just jumped out at me, I would put the Bible down or push it aside and open my journal.

I'd write down the passage and talk to the Lord about what I had just read.

My journal entries become a permanent record of an intimate conversation I have had with God. It is also where I write down my prayer requests. Then when I look back on the entries, it is amazing to see God's hand in my life—how He orchestrates opportunities, diverts me from danger, and answers prayers.

When I write something in my journal and intentionally give God time to respond to a question or issue I had on my heart, the answers from Him reveal how much He cares about me and my concerns.

The book of John begins with these words: *In the beginning was the Word, and the Word was with God, and the Word was God.*

When we read the Bible, we are truly hearing God's voice, understanding His thoughts, and feeling His heart. Journaling my thoughts and any revelation I am given really allows me to have an intimate interaction with El Shaddai, God Almighty.

He can hide us under His wings as we spend intimate time with Him, because that's what He desires.

When the Word says that He is a jealous God, He's jealous for our attention. He wants intimacy, and He doesn't want to share that intimacy with anything or anyone else.

With practice, journaling will become a time where you can meet God as you pour out your heart and allow Him to pour into you. You really can have a two-way conversation with God, the One who knows your heart better than you know it yourself.

It was through those intimate moments that God taught me some of the most valuable lessons of my life. But first He embarked upon a mission to restore what had been taken from me since I was young child. I must often reclaim power and authority that I have surrendered to the enemy as God reveals His truths to me during my devotions and intercessory prayer times with Him.

CHAPTER 17

Restoring Relationships

Then He who sat on the throne said, "Behold, I make all things new."
And He said to me, "Write, for these words are true and faithful." And
He said to me, "It is done! I am the Alpha and the Omega, the Beginning
and the End. I will give of the fountain of the water of life freely to him
who thirsts. He who overcomes shall inherit all things, and I will be his
God and he shall be My son."

—Rev. 21:5–7

Even before I accepted Christ as my Lord and Savior, I knew I was a seeker. I was looking for something but didn't quite know what it was. I never experienced any period of emotional settling until I realized that Christ was the answer and that He was at the core of my longing.

I began to pursue Him on a more fervent basis to form a real relationship. Yes, He saved me from the penalty of sin when I asked Him to be my Lord and Savior. Understanding what His lordship meant and exploring that relationship gave me an entirely new perspective on life.

For the first time, I began to understand what true love is and how it is defined in a whole different way than what I had experienced growing up. It's not filled with conditions. It's not filled with a threat that if I don't do things the right way, then I deserve to be punished. Growing up, that's how love was defined to me emotionally.

Christ is consistent with His love regardless of how I feel or how I act. I can always turn to Him for comfort. Initially this concept was so foreign to me that when I started to experience Christ's love, I began to doubt it. "It cannot be that simple," I thought.

After a while, I came to realize that I couldn't evaluate Christ's love for me based on what I had experienced in my own life. Christ's love couldn't be based on the traditions or the belief patterns that were instilled in me growing up. I just had to abandon that punishment-reward way of thinking, and start fresh.

I began building a brand-new foundation for my life from scratch. I had to discover what it truly means to be a Christian. The starting point required reshaping of my identity. I had to battle a spiritual tug-of-war, especially in my twenties. I was looking for other people to help define who I was. Truthfully, they didn't have a clue.

I tried to associate with people who I felt had arrived much earlier on their faith journey or with those who simply seemed to be a little bit more confident regarding who they are. I thought maybe they could teach me how to be who I am. It never occurred to me to ask my Creator to show me who He created me to be.

Being a Christian is about relationship with Jesus Christ (Son), God (Father), and the Holy Spirit. I needed a relationship on all three levels.

After I came to see myself as God sees me, my perspective changed in many ways.

One of the first changes occurred in the way I saw my mother. We had never been close growing up, and I sometimes wondered if she resented having me based on the way she talked about my father. From adolescence into early adulthood, a healthy emotional perspective for me was a relentless pursuit outside of my family.

I don't want to dishonor my mother, because she did the very best that she knew how. The reality is that people who have been abused and neglected may become abusive at times, especially emotionally abusive. It's the concept that "hurting people" hurt others.

She gave what she knew to give. She didn't know how to help me build a good, healthy emotional self-esteem.

Luke 6:45 explains it this way: *A good man out of the good treasure of his heart brings forth good; and an evil man out of the evil treasure of his heart brings forth evil. For out of the abundance of the heart his mouth speaks.*

Ma certainly was not evil. She battled with the same self-esteem issues I did. Fortunately I had Christ whispering to me in a loving language, encouragement about who I really am as a person. My hope is that Ma will come to know God as a loving Father, Christ as the beloved Redeemer, and Holy Spirit as the ultimate Guide and Comforter.

I think Ma is now on a spiritual journey herself. She is such a strong woman that as she gains access to God's heart, she'll have tremendous influence on many people around her. She will have such peace in her life when she discovers that God really, truly loves her despite all the things she regrets doing. The joy will overflow in her heart when Jesus heals her. It's one of my most fervent prayers.

Ma tried to block me reconnecting with my father. She planted a lot of negative seeds. She once said, "You need to be careful about staying with those people who you don't know. Who's to say if their home is safe?"

I chose to ignore those statements, and pressed forward.

After my faith deepened, I came to understand that she was just trying to protect her heart. Perhaps she thought that if I established a relationship with my father, I would discover an embarrassing or painful memory from her past that she wanted hidden.

My faith journey has really opened my eyes to my father's situation too. For a very long time, I felt like there was this huge secret associated with my birth. It was almost as though it was a shameful event. In fact, I was prompted to take a DNA test with my father to confirm his paternity.

When I reconciled with my father and connected with my paternal family, Ma stopped vocalizing her negative opinion to me, but she still spoke ill of me and Randolph to others.

Reuniting with him was as though the pieces of a giant jigsaw puzzle were finally coming together. I saw that he and I have similar personalities and tastes.

Randolph was living a life as a single man. He was in Milwaukee with a few family members nearby. He has a lot of friends, but most of them are considerably older than he is. They became like a pseudo-family to him, just like my friends became a family for me.

Randolph has done everything possible to avoid speaking negatively of Ma or Daddy. I love that! It is as though he doesn't want to come between me and the other important people in my life. He has occasionally asked about my siblings and parents and encourages me to steward those relationships.

Unfortunately he has been shackled in bondage to guilt and shame for abandoning me and for not being involved in my life. The guilt is so deep that even reassurances that I forgive him don't matter. He may understand I forgive him, but I think he still harbors a belief that God never could forgive him for decisions he made. He internalizes that guilt and turns to alcohol to numb the pain.

I sense God is also working on him through his association with me. My father and I can reclaim lost years through a positive relationship today. While he may not have been in my life to help guide me as a child, teen, or young adult, he is willing to provide fatherly love and wisdom now.

Lesson Learned: Don't Judge People Too Quickly.

There were times in my life where I perceived what a man's role ought to be. In other words, I expected him to live up to a standard I set for him that was much higher than he could ever attain on his own. I was working to shape him into a man of my own creation, rather than allowing God to shape him as He intended. God told me that I needed to understand my relationship with Him before I could even attempt to discern another person's heart. Just as He defines who I am and who I ought to be, I need to be comfortable knowing that He's undertaking the same process in others too.

God has told me, "Let me define how your husband's covering will be or that of certain men I put in your life, whether they be spiritual fathers, mentors, friends, family, or bosses. Let me reveal to you what their covering may be."

Photo 10: Celebrating my birthday with friends and family in a new home I purchased in Georgia

CONCLUSION

For I know the thoughts that I think toward you, says the Lord, thoughts of peace and not of evil, to give you a future and a hope.

—Jer. 29:11

My life started out with trauma, but I know I will finish strong.

God made promises to me that remain unfulfilled, but I can trust Him in knowing that He is always faithful to do what He promises.

In this next era of my life, I have great expectations of what the Christian experience will be. I know I am perfect only through my abiding relationship in Christ. For my heavenly Father has taken great pleasure in me.

Yes, I have endured a great deal of pain, as well as joy, in my life. It is my prayer that through my experience, you can find hope and healing for the things that hurt you and people who have wounded you.

I leave you with one of my favorite Bible passages: *These things I have spoken to you, that in Me you may have peace. In the world you will have tribulation; but be of good cheer, I have overcome the world* (John 16:33). Whatever has kept you down, rest assured that with God's help, you can overcome your past and embrace a glorious future!

Terrina Wilder
January 2021

ABOUT THE AUTHOR

Terrina Wilder has pursued purpose in her personal and professional life since the age of sixteen. Her military career opened opportunities for her in v a r i o u s industries, such as healthcare, veterinary medicine, drug development, and chemical/medical device manufacturing.

In addition to journaling, in her spare time, Terrina enjoys living in the North Texas area where she can be found participating in outdoor excursions, training aspiring regulatory and quality professionals, and serving her local community through trade organizations and prayer/deliverance ministries.

Ms. Wilder is passionate about investing in the younger generation to be an example of conforming to one's true identity and fulfilling a life of purpose.

Other literary work of Terrina Wilder include a featured short story in a Christmas Anthology called, *'Tis the Season: A Holiday Anthology: 2020 Season.* Expect to see more Christian fiction and non-fiction writings from this exceptional author.

www.ingramcontent.com/pod-product-compliance
Lightning Source LLC
Chambersburg PA
CBHW021825090426
42811CB00032B/2023/J